Charles T Loehr

War history of the old First Virginia Infantry Regiment

Army of Northern Virginia

Charles T Loehr

War history of the old First Virginia Infantry Regiment
Army of Northern Virginia

ISBN/EAN: 9783743312388

Manufactured in Europe, USA, Canada, Australia, Japa

Cover: Foto ©ninafisch / pixelio.de

Manufactured and distributed by brebook publishing software
(www.brebook.com)

Charles T Loehr

War history of the old First Virginia Infantry Regiment

WAR HISTORY

OF THE

Old First Virginia Infantry Regiment,

ARMY OF NORTHERN VIRGINIA,

BY CHARLES T. LOEHR.

Published by Request of the Old First Virginia Infantry Association.

RICHMOND:
WM. ELLIS JONES, BOOK AND JOB PRINTER.
1884.

INTRODUCTION.

The following sketch of the career of the "Old First," during the war, is derived from a diary and the personal recollections of the writer; use also is made of written statements of some of his comrades. The writer knows full well that he cannot do justice to the laurels won by the "Old First," but he hopes that this will be the means of inciting some one more able than he to write and publish the record of events partly herein described.

It was the writer's peculiar good luck to have been able to verify in person all the scenes he describes; he participated in all the battles and marches of the regiment, from its muster into service of the State, April, 1861, to the battle of Five Forks, April, 1865, where he was taken prisoner.

These lines are intended to perpetuate the part which the Old First Virginia infantry took in the war, and they are dedicated to the memory of his lamented friend and comrade, Major George Fisher Norton.

CHARLES T. LOEHR,

Secretary of the Old First Va. Infantry Ass'n,
and formerly Sergeant of Co. "D."

RICHMOND, *February, 1884.*

WAR HISTORY

OF THE

Old First Virginia Infantry Regiment.

On the 17th day of April, 1861, Virginia issued the proclamation of secession, and the clouds which long since had gathered black and blacker over this country broke; the pen was declared useless, and it was left to the sword to settle the issues and contentions agitating the political parties of these States. But I am not going to write as to the causes of the war, but simply to state some of the events constituting a part of the history of the Old First Virginia infantry regiment—a regiment of which the citizens of Richmond had every reason to be justly proud.

In March, 1861, I, with many of my young Richmond friends, organized a company, which was known as the "Old Dominion Guard." Joseph G. Griswold was elected Captain, and William H. Palmer First, and Henry Harney Second Lieutenants. Soon we had over eighty men together, and by constant drilling, and the interest we took in being soldiers, the company made a splendid appearance. On the 20th we went into barracks, on Main, between Seventh and Eighth streets—that is, we got a lot of straw piled on the upper floor of the building where we slept. Not very comfortable the first night, but then it was something new. The next day we were mustered into service of the State of Virginia by General Baldwin, and commenced to do duty. Part of the company was sent to take charge of the custom house, and a part to Rocketts to stand guard over the steamers. A few days after this we were attached to the First regiment of Virginia volunteers, as Company "D."

THE FIRST REGIMENT OF VIRGINIA VOLUNTEERS.

The First regiment Virginia volunteers was organized May 1st, 1851, in the city of Richmond, Virginia. Its first Colonel was Walter Gwynn ; it participated in the John Brown insurrection with full ranks, then under command of Colonel Thomas P. August. In 1860, P. T. Moore was elected Colonel of the regiment. Various companies, up to this time, had composed the regiment, most of which had but a brief existence. At the outbreak of the war the regiment was constituted as follows :

FIELD AND STAFF.

P. T. Moore, .	. *Colonel.*
William H. Fry, .	*Lieutenant-Colonel.*
William Munford, . .	. *Major.*
Samuel P. Mitchell,	*Adjutant.*
Dr. J. S. D. Cullen,	. *Surgeon.*
T. F. Maury, . . .	*Assistant Surgeon.*
Lieutenant W. G. Allan,	. *Quartermaster.*
Captain D. B. Bridgeford, .	*Commissary.*
J. Adair Pleasants, .	. *Paymaster.*

NON-COMMISSIONED STAFF.

William O. Harvie, .	. *Sergeant-Major.*
C. E. Gronwald, .	. *Quartermaster-Sergeant.*
E. P. Hudgins, .	*Commissary-Sergeant.*
E. P. Reeve, .	. *Ensign.*

BAND.

James B. Smith, (leader—13 pieces), *Captain.*

DRUM CORPS.

C. R. M. Pohle (14 drummers), . . *Drum-Major.*

COMPANIES.

Co.	NAME OF COMPANY.	ORGANIZED.	CAPTAINS.
A,	Richmond Grays,	June 18, 1844,	Wyatt M. Elliott.
B,		April 12, 1861,	James K. Lee.
C,	Montgomery Guard,	Sept. 1849,	John Dooley.
D,	Old Dominion Guard,	March 1861,	Joseph G. Griswold.
E,	Richmond L't Infantry Blues,	May 10, 1793,	O. Jennings Wise.
F,		Oct. 19, 1859,	R. Milton Cary.
G,		Aug. 1859,	William H. Gordon.
H,	Second Company Grays,	April 1861,	Francis J. Boggs.
I,		Nov. 19, 1859,	R. F. Morris.
K,	Virginia Rifles,	March 1, 1850,	Florence Miller.

About the middle of April, three companies were detached. Company A (the Grays) was sent to Norfolk, where it was afterwards attached to the Twelfth Virginia regiment. Company E, (the Blues,) and Company F, were sent to Fredericksburg and assigned to other commands. Several efforts were made to get these companies back to the regiment, but without result. In regard to Company E (Blues), and Company F, we find the following, from Daniel Ruggles, in command at Fredericksburg, writing to General R. S. Garnett, Adjutant-General Virginia forces, under date of May 24th, 1861:

SIR:

 I have the honor to state, in answer to the communication from the Commanding General of the forces, dated the 13th instant, that I cannot spare the two companies from Richmond (Captains Wise's and Cunningham's), without irreparable injury to the service, for some time to come. These companies, under the command of Colonel Cary, are now—in conjunction with other forces—covering the Potomac batteries and avenues of approach, becoming acquainted with the character of the district and its natural defences, thus rendering their services indispensable.

I have also to state (on information) that the officers and men in said companies are anxious to remain here, to be incorporated with a regiment about to be organized. Their return to Richmond, it is said, would give the greatest dissatisfaction, and very probably break up these fine companies.

Thus we had but seven companies, until the middle of July, just before the battle of Bull Run, a company from Washington, D. C., commanded by Captain Sherman, was attached to the regiment as Company E, and at Centreville another company, Captain Shafer's, also from Washington, was temporarily attached as Company F.

On the 27th of April the regiment marched to the new Fair Grounds, then known as "Camp of Instruction." Here our first tents were pitched, and camp life commenced in earnest. Drilling and standing guard soon became familiar to us. Sundays usually found the camp deserted. On one occasion there was only one man in Company D left to "fall in." When the drum beat for dinner, the Captain, who was in his tent, called out, "Fall in, Company D," to which the one man replied, "Captain, must we form in one, or two ranks?" to which the reply came, "Of course, in two ranks." When the Captain came out of his tent he found Private Craig standing alone, with his legs far apart, as he said, in two ranks.

On the 24th of May, orders came for us to leave, on the next day, for Manassas.

On the 25th, the regiment struck tents and formed into line. Hundreds of ladies and members of the soldiers' families were present to bid us farewell. Every musket was adorned with a bouquet of flowers. At the gate a train of cars was waiting, and under the strains of old Smith's band we embarked on board. Everywhere on the route the ladies were assembled. At Ashland, Fredericks Hall, Tolersville and Louisa Courthouse we stopped a short while, accepting the tokens of affection bestowed on us by Virginia's lovely daughters. Pincushions, flowers, cakes, &c., more than we could carry, were handed us, while our band played a gay tune, and everybody was happy. The next day we reached Manassas; things did not look quite so lovely there, for only a small force was as yet assembled, and matters looked quite gloomy.

The camp was known as "Camp Pickens," under charge of General Bonham, who was relieved some time in June, by General Beauregard. Marching about half a mile north of Manassas, we pitched our tents on a hill west of the railroad.

On the 29th we were treated to a false alarm, and had a march to Bull Run. The long-roll beat to arms, and men hurried from all points to their camps. After forming in the company streets, muskets were loaded, and the line of march was taken up for Centreville. We crossed Bull Run at Mitchell's Ford, and met a number of citizens and ladies in carriages, hurrying within our lines. Soon after passing Mitchell's Ford, information was received that no enemy was advancing, and we were ordered back to Manassas. Arriving at our camps, we were formed in close column and had a rousing address from General Bonham.

On the evening of the 1st of June, Companies B, D, G and K, were ordered to Fairfax Courthouse, under the command of Major William Munford, arriving there after a night's march from Fairfax Station, which we reached by the cars. There had been quite a sharp skirmish on the 1st, in which Captain Marr, of the Warrenton Rifles, was killed. Here we did outpost duty, sleeping in an old barn and getting up every morning at dawn expecting to meet the enemy. This lasted until the 21st, when we left the post to some South Carolina troops, without regret, and marched back to our comfortable quarters at Manassas.

One of the features of our camp life was our regimental dress-parade, the regiment making a splendid appearance. In the manual of arms it could not be surpassed—the whole line moved like a machine; and then our fine band and drum corps added to the display. We usually had many spectators, among them General Beauregard and staff could be seen on most occasions.

On the 17th of July orders came to meet the enemy, who was then advancing from Washington. This time it was no false alarm. We marched to Bull Run, crossed at Blackburn's Ford, and halted during the night on the north bank of the Run. On the morning of the 18th we re-crossed the Run, and formed in line of battle, and were placed in position as follows: Our company (D) was deployed as skirmishers, occupying the right of the line on the Run; Company E (Sherman's) to our left, and covering the crossing at Blackburn's Ford; the left of this company rested on Company K, which adjoined the Seventeenth Virginia Regiment; and next was the Eleventh Virginia Regiment, all under the command of General Longstreet. Some of the companies of these regiments participated in the fight; the rest of our regiment (with the exception of Company I, which arrived towards the close of the battle took position on Company D's right.) Companies B, C, G and H formed in the field in our rear. About 11 o'clock the enemy opened with artillery, which was replied to by the Washington Artillery, of New Orleans, posted in the open field in our rear, and Kemper's Battery further to the left, near Mitchell's Ford. The artillery-firing lasted until 1 o'clock, when we could hear the bugles of the enemy's skirmish lines blow for the charge. The attack was made in the centre of our regimental line. The Companies B, C, G and H, that were held in reserve, were then sent forward, and fought (mingled with the companies who had been formed as skirmishers) for some time on the bank of the stream. When the enemy's fire slackened, these reserve companies were ordered across the Run, where the enemy was met in heavy force. Here among the trees on the side of the hill the principal part of the fighting was done. Our colors, carried by Ensign E. P. Reeve, marked the position of our charging columns through the powder smoke which enveloped the hill. Colonel P. T. Moore was struck down, and Major F. G. Skinner took command, and by his daring and cool manner, won the confidence and esteem of the regiment.*   For nearly two hours the battle lasted, when the enemy was forced to fall back, and the regiment was relieved by the Seventh Virginia. The storm of lead and iron passed through our ranks for the first time, but the men stood it like they were used to it all their lives.   But many a poor fellow was laid low; five were buried the next morning under an apple-tree, several more died afterwards, and about twenty-five, more or less, wounded.

LIST OF CASUALTIES.

Field and Staff.—Wounded: Colonel P. T. Moore, Quartermaster Captain W. G. Allen.

Company B.—Killed: Captain James K. Lee; Private John E. Allen.   Wounded: Lieutenant W. W. Harrison; Sergeants W. J. Lumpkin and J. Henry Cobb; Privates Fred. Lutz, Nat Kesler.

Company C.—Killed: Sergeant Pat. Rankin; Privates Mike Redmond and James Driscol.   Wounded: Lieutenant William English; Sergeant Joseph L. Whittaker; Privates Andrew W. Forsight, Michael Hughes, John Hamilton and John Kavanaugh.

Company E.—Killed: Corporal Isidore Morrice; Private J. E. Moran.   Wounded: Privates Thomas Collins, and Ph. K. Reiley.

Company G.—Killed: Lieutenant Humphrey H. Miles; Privates Scott J. Mallory and Southney S. Wilkinson.   Wounded: Privates Henry Ashby, George F. Knauff, William S. Ware, Benjamin H. Hord, and James A. Royster; Corporal Robert A. Crump.

Company H.—Killed: Private Milton A. Barnes.   Wounded: Privates John A. Morgan, R. S. Betts, and W. B. Eggleston.

Company K.—Killed: Privates Wolfgang Diacont and Frederick Gutbier.   Wounded: Privates Henry Duebel, William E. Cree, and A. Hatke.

Killed and died from wounds, 13; wounded, 27—40.

---

* Major F. G. Skinner was highly complimented for his gallant conduct by General Longstreet. He had been with us but a short while, having been assigned to the position as Major in place of William Munford, who left us for some other command. A few weeks afterwards Lieutenant-Colonel W. H. Fry resigned, and Major Skinner was promoted to this position, and Captain John Dooley, of Company C, was promoted Major.

General Longstreet reported the total loss of this battle at sixty-eight, including fifteen killed. It will, therefore, be seen that the principal loss in this action fell on our regiment.

The enemy engaged consisted of a part of Tyler's Division, Richardson's Brigade, and the First Massachusetts, Second and Third Michigan and Twelfth New York Regiments. Ayers' Battery and Brackett's Cavalry are named. They reported nineteen killed, thirty-eight wounded and twenty-six captured in the brigade. Mention is also made of a battalion of light infantry as being engaged.

General James Longstreet, who commanded the brigade to which our regiment belonged, at the battle of Bull Run, writes, under date of July 20th, 1883, in reply to an invitation to attend our annual reunion, as follows:

The old First Regiment was with me at Bull Run on the 18th of July, and made the first fight of Bull Run, which drove the Federals and forced them around Sudley Springs. This move on their part was the cause of delay that gave us time to draw our troops down from the Valley, and concentrate for the fight of the 21st. The heavy part of this fight was made by the old First Regiment, so that it can well claim to have done more towards the success of the First Manassas than any one regiment. This, too, was their first battle, and I can say that its officers and men did their duties as well, if not better, than any troops whose service came under my observation.

At night we marched about a mile in the rear to rest. Other of our troops occupied the battle-field. The next day General Beauregard rode by, and enquiring the name of the regiment, upon being told it was the First Virginia, exclaimed, "And a noble regiment it is."

On the 20th we resumed our position at Blackburn's Ford. The morning of the 21st opened with the distant thunder of cannon. On this day the battle of Manassas was fought and won. The fighting was to the left of our position, but we were severely exposed to artillery fire all day, losing six men wounded, as follows:

Field and Staff.—Major F. G. Skinner.

Company D.—Privates E. R. Miller, J. T. Porter and D. S. Edwards.

Company K.—Privates Adam Diacont and C. P. Degenhart.

At one time orders came for us to charge a battery, but after getting across the Run the command was countermanded. In the evening the welcome news came, "The enemy is routed." We crossed the Run again to follow the flying enemy towards Centreville, but were halted on the way. Right here nearly the whole Southern army formed one solid mass—over 30,000 men. "Onward, after them," was the cry, but it came otherwise. As far as we could see were the deserted camps of the enemy. Cracker-boxes, cooking-utensils, and everything most were strewn over the ground. After halting a short while we again recrossed Bull Run, and at 2 A. M. halted to camp on its southern bank.

The next day I, with some others of my company, visited the battle-field of Manassas. It was a sight that made me sick. Rows of dead, like flowers from a distance, looked the New York Zouaves, all dressed in red. They were burying the dead by dragging the bodies into shallow ditches and shoveling a few spadefuls of earth on them. At the Henry House lay an old lady, also killed, and all the houses were filled with the wounded.

Then for two days it rained, and everywhere the mud was knee-deep. War was no longer funny.

On the 24th we marched to Centreville. On the route we found all the houses and churches filled with the enemy's wounded, abandoned in the rapid flight on the 21st. Reaching Centreville that evening, we went into camp, resuming drill, guard-duty, &c. Captain Shafer's company, from Washington—about 60 men—was added to the regiment as Company F. This company, however, left us again at Fairfax Courthouse, after a stay of about six or eight weeks.

A few days after our arrival at Centreville, Prince Jerome Napoleon came through the lines, and the army was drawn up in line for his inspection. Our regiment had the special honor of passing in review before him. He remarked to Major Skinner, he supposed we were the Confederate Regulars, saying our marching and appearance seemed to him perfect, but thought our uniforms were somewhat in need of repairs (which was true). Major Skinner replied (pointing to us), "Those men you see were all, a few months ago, clerks or mechanics from Richmond," which the Prince would hardly believe; and as to the uniforms, the Major remarked, they (meaning us) have not given the enemy a chance to observe their rears. Prince Napoleon looked like a fat, jolly fellow; had on a black suit, white vest, and wore a straw hat. What his mission was has never been explained.

August 10th, we marched to Fairfax Courthouse, about seven miles off, and formed a camp on the south side of that town, which was called Camp Harrison. While here we were paid off, and the accompanying schedule shows the strength of the regiment:

ABSTRACT

From the Muster Roll of August, 1861, at Camp Harrison, Fairfax Courthouse, Va.

Companies.	PRESENT AND ABSENT.						PRESENT FOR DUTY.					
	Captains.	Lieutenants.	Sergeants.	Corporals.	Privates.	Total.	Captains.	Lieutenants.	Sergeants.	Corporals.	Privates.	Total.
B	1	3	4	4	67	79	1	1	3	4	49	58
C	1	3	4	4	86	98	1	2	2	4	74	83
D	1	3	4	4	78	90	1	3	4	4	69	81
E *	1	3	4	4	64	76	1	2	3	4	44	54
G	1	3	4	4	78	90	1	3	4	4	67	79
H	1	3	4	4	80	92	1	2	4	4	65	76
I	1	3	4	4	57	69	1	3	3	4	52	63
K	1	3	4	4	75	87	1	3	4	4	64	76
	8	24	32	32	585	681	8	19	27	32	484	570

* Sherman's company, from Washington, D. C.

Aggregate Strength of the Regiment.

Commissioned Staff,	6
Non-commissioned Staff,	5
Band,	13
Drummers,	14
Rank and file,	681
Total,	719

On the 14th we were sent to Falls Church for outpost duty, returning the next day. On the 26th we were again ordered to

Falls Church—which, by the way, was a very neat village, having two fine churches—but its inhabitants had fled, and not a man was seen in the deserted houses where we took our quarters for the night. To the north of Falls Church is Munson's Hill, which was captured by our men on the day previous to our arrival. From this hill a splendid view of Washington and its surrounding heights could be had. Colonel J. E. B. Stuart was in command here, having charge of the outpost service. The next morning our company was sent to the left of Munson's Hill, where we found Companies K and F engaged on the skirmish line. Halting in rear awhile, a howitzer was brought up, and after a few rounds we were ordered to charge the hill in our front (Febre's), and succeeded in driving the enemy's skirmishers therefrom, capturing a new drum, and later in the evening, two prisoners.

The following day there was a balloon ascension by the enemy near Alexandria, which, however, terminated rather abruptly, when the balloon was used for target practice by one of our rifled cannons, served by Captain Rosser's Washington Artillery, of New Orleans, who made some very fine shots, causing the balloon to descend in double-quick time.

On the 30th we returned to our camp. A few weeks afterwards the regiment was sent to Mason's Hill, where a part of our company was engaged in assisting a surveying expedition towards Alexandria, under command of Lieutenant G. F. Norton, and in coming back had quite a lively skirmish near Mason's Hill. During our stay at Fairfax Courthouse the city of Richmond furnished the whole regiment with new uniforms, otherwise nothing much of interest occurred, to mention, except constant picket, guard duty and drilling.

On the 16th of October we moved back to Centreville, where we prepared our winter quarters by adding chimneys to our tents. We had no other quarters during this winter, which proved to be exceedingly cold. Doing picket duty, sleeping in the snow and rain, in the wet woods or fields, throwing up earthworks, was a duty not much desired.

On the 28th of February, 1862, while the regiment was out on picket duty, we had a regular hurricane; all the fences were blown down and the night was intensely cold. When we returned to the camp, we found all our tents leveled except one or two, and our chimneys, consisting of flour barrels, had entirely disappeared.

The command of the regiment devolved for the most part on Major John Dooley, who, though not much of a military genius, was one of the kindest and most generous of men. Often on a bitter, cold night, he could be seen bringing the men on guard a drink, saying with a smile: "Boys, I saw you wink at me." On one occasion Sergeant Morris, of Company G, reported some of the men of his company as having gone to Richmond without leave. To which the Major replied: "And have they? the bad fellows! Let me know when they come back, and I will punish them severely." A few days after the Sergeant reported that they had returned. "Have they come back? the good fellows!" was the Major's remark, and that was about the last of that.

On brigade drill one day, we had to get over a line of breast-works and form into line on the other side. Colonel Skinner jumped his horse over, but Major Dooley looked on and smilingly remarked to the Colonel: "Just see how I do that." And the way he did it was by riding about a quarter of a mile along the line until he found an opening, when coming around he rode up to the Colonel, saying: "Did I not do that elegantly?"

A good many men left the regiment, some on furlough, others were detailed,* and the regiment, which numbered over 700 men, was reduced to less than 300.

On March 8th, 1862, the evacuation of Centreville took place. Our tents were struck, and all that could not be carried away was burned, while we ourselves, loaded like pack-mules, took up the line of march. We did not get farther, however, that day than about two and a half miles, owing to some obstructions in the road, and halted for the night in the woods. Started again

---

*The seat of Government being removed to Richmond, and most of the men of the regiment having a mercantile or mechanical education, contractors and those in charge of the Confederate offices were daily making applications to the War Department for some member of the regiment to fill positions of trust, or where mechanical skill was needed. As a rule the request was granted, and thus the Confederate War Department detailed the men faster than the officers could get new recruits. It became at last discouraging to the officers, and all the efforts of the commanders in the field failed to correct the evil. The need of such men at the capital was given as the excuse.

the next morning, and crossed the celebrated stone bridge at Bull Run, which was blown up that night after the army had crossed. Got to Gainesville that night; left there on the morning of the 10th; passed Buckland and New Baltimore; arrived at Warrenton at dark, passed through the town, and halted one mile beyond, completely worn out. Most of the men commenced to throw away part of their baggage, being unable to carry their loads. Started again the next morning, passing Amisville and Waterloo, and marching sixteen miles without a rest. At 10 P. M. halted in the Blue Ridge mountains, where we overtook our wagons and got three days' rations.

The next morning (the 12th) at 8 o'clock we were again on the road, passing Gaines' Cross Roads, Washington and Sperryville, in Rappahannock county, and stopped for the night near Woodville, having marched over seventeen miles. At 9 A. M. the next day we started again. The men were dropping out the ranks and straggling along the road, most of them being unused to this kind of marching. On the 14th we reached Hazel Run, where we rested, allowing the stragglers to come up. Weather very bad, raining all night and all day, and we were all wet to the skin.

On the second evening after our arrival in this dreary place, Major Dooley had the regiment drawn up, and gave the following verbal instructions: "Men, you must not go to the wagon-yard, or any other place of amusement. Parade dismissed!"

On the 16th we started again, crossed Hazel Run, and halted within two miles of Culpeper Courthouse for the night. On the next morning (the 17th) we passed through Culpeper Courthouse, marched about seven miles, and encamped. The roads were in a miserable condition, and our wagons could not go fast. Started again the next morning, crossed the Rapidan river, and halted near Orange Courthouse. The roads were in a horrible condition, the mud in some places being two feet deep, and the wagons frequently got stuck. Halted here for three days, during which time it rained almost continuously.

On the 22d passed through Orange Courthouse, the streets of which presented a perfect swamp. After marching about a mile, we camped on Dr. Taylor's farm until the 3d of April. Moved at night in direction of Fredericksburg, marching about nine miles. On the 4th passed Vidiersville, and halted on the road that night. On the 5th we turned off this road, started in a southern direction, halting at Macedonia Church. The next day we reached Louisa Courthouse. For two days there was a constant snow, hail and rain storm, and the country roads over which we passed were nothing but a bed of soft mud. At Louisa Courthouse General A. P. Hill, in command of the brigade, treated the men to a drink of whiskey at his own expense.

On the 8th, left Louisa Courthouse and halted near Tolersville, on Mountain Road. The next day marched twenty miles to Brick Store, on the 10th to Ground Squirrel Church, Hanover county, and on the 12th stopped at Young's Mill Pond, where we remained till the 16th, when we marched through Richmond and embarked on the steamer "Glen Cove," in the evening, reaching King's Mill wharf at 2 A. M. on the 17th. Rested on the river bank till 9 A. M., then marched to Winn's Mill, where we halted. The next day, the 18th, took position in line of works, doing picket duty and strengthening the works. The enemy's line was about 1,000 yards distant, and we were exposed under severe shelling. In the rear of our line were some log cabins, put up for winter quarters. During a heavy rain some of our men got in one of these cabins for shelter, when one of the enemy's shells struck the cabin and exploded therein, killing Corporal E. M. Ferneyhough and wounding Private M. J. Wingfield, both from Company D. Ferneyhough was the first man our company lost; he was a brave and noble fellow, and his death was a cause of universal regret.

On the 24th, relieved by the Ninth Alabama, and camped near Lebanon Church. On the 21st our time of service expired, but as the country could not spare us just then, we held on to our occupation. A general reorganization, however, took place, and on the 26th new officers were elected as follows:

LEWIS B. WILLIAMS, Colonel.
FREDERICK G. SKINNER, Lieutenant-Colonel.
WILLIAM H. PALMER, Major.
T. HERBERT DAVIS, Captain Company B.
JAMES MITCHELL, Captain Company C.
GEORGE F. NORTON, Captain Company D.
FRANK H. LANGLEY, Captain Company G.
WILLIAM E. TYSINGER, Captain Company H.
J. W. TABB, Captain Company I.

Companies E and K, whose time of service had expired, disbanded, and most of the men joined other commands.

On the evening of the 3d of May, the evacuation of Yorktown commenced. Left the trenches during that night and halted about four or five miles in the rear, near an old church, for a short time, during which the reports of the ammunition and ordnance being blown up at Yorktown, could be distinctly heard. Marching part of that night and the next day, we reached Williamsburg, and halted on the west of that town, on the morning of the 4th, near the asylum. On the morning of the 5th our brigade, commanded by General A. P. Hill, was ordered to prepare for battle. It was a wet, rainy day. At about 10 o'clock A. M., we marched back through the city at double-quick time, and formed into line to the right of Fort Magruder, in an open field. An hour afterward we were sent into the woods, in front of which was cut down timber, forming an abattis.

We were ordered to support a Mississippi regiment, engaged heavily with the enemy. Before we could reach them, five companies broke and came through our ranks in confusion. The pursuit through the abattis threw the enemy into confusion, and our firm line and steady fire did great execution. We followed through the abattis, and beyond charged a battery of six guns, capturing it, and a large and a small battle flag. An aide of General Longstreet ordered Colonel Williams to detail one hundred men to bring these guns off, but Colonel Williams told him he could not spare this force; whereupon a detail of the Nineteenth Virginia regiment was obtained, which carried the guns to the rear.

The fact of Colonel Williams' inability to furnish the men to carry off these guns led to some controversy, which was, however, decided in favor of our regiment. Below are two communications published at that time, one in the *Whig* and the other in the *Dispatch*, of May 12th and 25th, 1862, respectively.*

---

*"CORRECTION" CORRECTED.

HEADQUARTERS FIRST REG'T VIRGINIA VOLUNTEERS,
CAMP ON BODEKER'S FARM, *May 24th, 1862.*

To the Editor of the Whig:

The *Enquirer* of the 23d contains a communication signed "A. B. C., 28th Va. Reg't," in which the writer states that "A report has been

After this successful charge we crossed an open field before us, and halted in the edge of a piece of woods. Here we became separated from the brigade, and during the balance of the day the regiment fought on its own hook. Seeing the Federal lines pass

---

going the rounds of the Richmond press, that the First Virginia regiment charged and captured the Federal battery stationed on the main road leading from Williamsburg to King's Mill landing. This is erroneous. * * * No part of the First Virginia regiment was near this battery at any time during the action." The *Whig* of to-day (24th) contains a communication from Colonel J. B. Strange, Nineteenth Virginia regiment, headed "Correction," in which he states that the "issue of the 19th instant contains an editorial paragraph so grossly misrepresenting a part of the action of the 5th instant, near Williamsburg, in which my regiment is alluded to, I feel compelled, for the sake of truth as well as justice to the gallant band I commanded on that occasion, to correct your statement. You say that after the First Virginia regiment had captured a battery, Colonel Williams requested me to make a detail from my regiment to take it to the rear. You may infer my surprise at seeing this statement, when I inform you that *I was not present* at any battery captured by that regiment. * * * I asked Colonel Williams, who I discovered had come up on my left, to assist me in getting the pieces off, which he declined doing on account of the "smallness of his regiment." "A. B. C., 28th Va. Reg't," is answered by Colonel Strange of the Nineteenth. "A. B. C." (Twenty-eighth) says that "no part of the First Virginia was near the battery at any time during the action," and Colonel Strange says that "he had a conversation with Colonel Williams, who he discovered had come up on his left." The issue is simply one of veracity. Colonel Williams is wounded and a prisoner. When being borne from the field he said that the battery would be claimed by the Nineteenth Virginia, because, when the First Virginia passed through it, he had not men enough to take it off, and requested Colonel Strange to make a detail from his regiment to do so. The colors of the battery were placed on a caisson by a member of the First Virginia regiment. On the third day after the battle I had a conversation with Colonel Strange, in the presence of several witnesses, on the subject of the battery, and understood him to concede the fact that the First Virginia had taken it.

WILLIAM H. PALMER,
Major Commanding.

I was with the First Virginia regiment in an engagement near Williamsburg, on the 5th of May, and during that engagement we succeeded in capturing a battery from the enemy. The First Virginia had passed through said battery and formed line when the Nineteenth over the field in our rear, we fell back to the woods, from where we started. Here the fighting was continued. The balls appeared to come from all directions, while our regiment was without any support. Colonel L. B. Williams was badly wounded,

Virginia had crossed the road and formed on our right. Colonel Williams then requested Colonel Strange to send the battery to the rear, giving as a reason for applying to him, that the First had so few men he could not spare any for that purpose. Soon after Colonel Strange passed, with a few men and a flag from the Nineteenth on our right, to our left, where the guns were, and immediately afterwards all went into action and left the battery to our rear. Who took the guns off I cannot say, but the First Virginia was the first to clear it of live Federal soldiers.

JAMES W. TABB,
Captain Company I, First Virginia Regiment.

With regard to the above, I have only to state that when the battery on the main road was charged through and taken by the First Virginia regiment, Colonel Strange and his regiment had not come upon the ground. It was not until having obtained permission from Colonel Williams, I had made a detail from my company, of a Lieutenant and some men, for the purpose of manning one of the guns and turning it on the then retreating enemy, that they arrived, coming up on our right, when, as I then understood from Colonel Williams, he made arrangements with Colonel Strange for its removal. Any one who was on the field at that time will see the absurdity of the statement of " A. B. C.," Twenty-eighth Virginia, in his article in the *Enquirer* of the 23d instant.

JAMES MITCHEL,
Captain Company C, First Virginia Volunteers.

I was present at the capture of the battery spoken of in the foregoing article, and after the First Virginia regiment had passed through it and formed twenty steps beyond, Colonel Strange came from the right and said to Colonel Williams, by whose side I was standing, " Williams, you ought to send a detail to take that battery off the field," to which Colonel Williams replied, " Colonel, it is impossible for me to do it, as I have only one hundred and fifty men, but I wish you would do it." Colonel Strange then ordered the battery to be spiked, but eventually some of them were carried from the field by a detail from the Nineteenth regiment.

WILLIAM T. FRY,
First Lieut. and Adjutant First Reg't Va. Vols.

STATEMENTS OF AN EYE-WITNESS.

A gentleman who witnessed the fight near Williamsburg on Monday, informs us that our force engaged amounted to six or eight thousand

and carried off the field, after which Major W. H. Palmer, who had also been wounded, but did not leave the field, took charge, and under his gallant and daring leadership the men did their duty nobly on that trying day.

When night came the survivors made their way back to town. It had been raining all the time, and the men were completely broken down, after fighting all that day without being relieved. We lost eight men killed and about thirty wounded from the regiment:

Field and Staff.—Wounded: Colonel Lewis B. Williams* and Major William H. Palmer.

Company B.—Killed: Corporal Charles D. Beale; Privates —— Jordan and Peter Moss. Wounded: Privates Mungo P. Buchanan, John Jacobs, Jr.,* and Adam Smith.

Company C.—Killed: Private Patrick Keeting. Wounded: Private James H. Dooley.*

Company D.—Killed: Private George Logan. Wounded:

---

men. The battle lasted nine hours. The First Virginia regiment captured a battery of eight guns, and two colors, from the enemy. There has been some dispute in regard to which regiment performed this gallant act, but we learn that the matter has been decided in favor of the First by the General commanding the brigade to which it is attached. The number of casualties in killed and wounded in General A. P. Hill's brigade have been ascertained as follows· First regiment, 46; Seventh regiment, 90; Eleventh regiment, 131; Seventeenth regiment, 71; total, 338. Some erroneous statements have been published in connection with this battle, which we are now enabled to correct. General Early was not mortally wounded; his injuries are severe, but it is believed he will soon recover and be able to take the field again. Colonel Williams, of the First Virginia, received a very severe wound, and is now in the hands of the enemy. Major Palmer, of the same regiment, who was reported killed, received only a slight wound in the arm, and remained on the field until the close of the engagement. Neither Colonel Kemper nor Colonel Corse, both of whom were reported wounded, received any injury, though they exposed themselves in a daring manner throughout the day. The rumor that General Anderson was killed probably arose from the death of his brother, who fell in the battle. The General was not injured. We hear that the loss on our side, in killed, wounded and missing, is estimated at 500. The loss of the enemy can only be conjectured, though it was unquestionably much heavier than ours.

*Those marked * were left in the enemy's hands.

Lieutenant E. P. Reeve;* Sergeants L. M. Blanton and J. M. Finn; Privates T. H. Haley,* E. Priddy and D. S. Edwards. Prisoner: Private William H. Stewart.

Company G.—Killed: Sergeant C. C. Fowlks.   Wounded: Corporal A. J. Snead; Private H. B. Gary.

Company H.—Killed: Private Robert D. Swords.   Wounded: Captain W. E. Tysinger; Corporal Thomas S. Riddick; Privates C. P. Hansford, Edwin Gilham* and George A. Rae.

Company I.—Killed: Private John G. Grammer.   Wounded: Captain James W. Tabb; Lieutenant W. A. Caho; Sergeant R. M. Jones; Corporal C. L. Parker; Privates John T. Ayers, J. F. Devoux* and Thomas Senoir.

Killed, 8; wounded, 27, of which 8 were left in hands of enemy; prisoner, 1.   Total, 36.

We captured several hundred prisoners, and could have taken more, the woods being full of scattered Federals; but we could not trouble ourselves with them.   During the night the men took shelter in the vacant houses of the town and dried themselves.

Early on the morning of the 6th the army left Williamsburg. The roads were almost impassable—wagons, horses and even some of the men got stuck in the deep mud, and were only by great exertions liberated.   Reached Burnt Ordinary, seven miles distant, that night.   On the 7th left at 4 A. M.; halted in line of battle till dark, marched all night, and on the 8th we reached the Chickahominy river.   During all this time we were without anything to eat, except dry corn, or what we could gather on the way.   It was therefore quite a treat when we again got our hunger stilled by rations being served to us at this place.   On the 9th we reached Long Bridge and camped for six days, resting our weary bodies, and on the 15th we continued our retreat towards Richmond.   A fearful rain set in during the night, and we were almost swimming in the water the next morning.   On the 16th we halted to camp on Clark's farm, near Darbytown, where we remained until the 27th; we were then marched to Mechanicsville Turnpike, near Howard's Grove, where we encamped.

While in camp near Darbytown, General James L. Kemper (formerly Colonel of the Seventh Virginia) was placed in

---

* Those marked * were left in the enemy's hands.

charge of the brigade, which consisted of our regiment (the First Virginia); the Seventh Virginia, Colonel W. Tazewell Patton, killed at Gettysburg, and succeeded by Colonel C. C. Floweree; the Eleventh Virginia, Colonel Samuel Garland, killed at Boonsboro', and succeeded by David Funsten, Maurice S. Langhorne and Kirk Otey; the Twenty-fourth Virginia, Colonel William R. Terry, promoted to Brigadier-General, succeeding General Kemper (disabled for field duty at Gettysburg) in command of the brigade, whereupon Colonel Richard L. Maury was promoted to the command of the regiment; the Seventeenth Virginia, Colonel M. D. Corse, who was promoted to Brigadier-General and placed in charge of a brigade, taking the Seventeenth Virginia with him. Some time in November, 1862, the place of the Seventeenth was filled by the Third Virginia, Colonel Joseph Mayo, Jr.

By constant intercourse the men of this old brigade came to know and love each other. Standing together, shoulder to shoulder, facing the storm of lead and iron on so many battlefields, traveling together so many weary miles, from the swamps of North Carolina to the mountains of Pennsylvania, made them comrades and brothers indeed. Never, to my knowledge, was there the slightest discord or strife between the various regiments composing this brigade. An insult to a member of this brigade was an insult to be resented by every individual man of the brigade. Right or wrong, they would assist and stand by each other; one relying on the other with implicit faith—these were the "Kemper's men."

During the evening of the 30th a heavy rain storm set in, flooding the whole camp. We went to Colonel Skinner to get permission to go to Richmond, and the old Colonel expressed himself thus: "I can't give you all permission to go; but you all know well enough how to flank the guards." We took the hint, and with the exception of one or two men, the camp was soon deserted. The morning of the 31st, the brigade was called under arms. There were only a few of the First regiment present, and these were, for a while, placed with the Seventh Virginia. On the march to the battle-ground of Seven Pines most all the absentees reappeared and fell into ranks, and some brought their brothers and friends with them. Formed in line of battle about 1 P. M., and were placed to the right of the Williamsburg road, where we remained until 5 P. M., when we were sent in to relieve the troops then engaged.

After reaching an open field, the line of battle was formed. Our regiment being in front, it advanced over the open field and came to a temporary halt behind a big wood-pile. Coming out from the shelter of this friendly protection, and while marching in four ranks to the right, the regiment was suddenly subjected to a fearful fire of musketry, which swept the ranks, killing and wounding over one-third of our men before they could return the compliment. The rest got into the works and continued the fight until, with the aid of the balance of our brigade, the enemy was driven off. Most of the men spent the night in General Casey's headquarters, where they found quite a supply of refreshments, left by the enemy in their retreat, which were duly appreciated by us after the hot day's work.

It will not be amiss to relate an incident here. A few days prior to the fight orders had been issued to hold the men strictly accountable for their arms and ammunition. During this battle Private "Monk" Wingfield, from Company D, had his musket shattered into fragments by a piece of shell. When told to throw it away and pick up another (hundreds of them were lying about), he replied: "I am not going to pay fifteen dollars for my gun; I am going to carry it back to the ordnance wagon," which he did the next day, when he got another gun.

The loss of the regiment was as follows:

Field and Staff.—Drill Master Lieutenant Thomas H. Mercer, wounded.

Company B.—Killed: Lieutenant Francis M. Mann; Corporal L. H. Strom. Wounded: Captain T. H. Davis; Lieutenant J. A. Payne; Sergeants J. L. Littlepage, W. Harper Dean; Corporals N. T. Ernest, William Carter, G. G. Goddin, William A. Stoaber; Privates George R. Heath, Fred. Loehr, R. J. Pollard.

Company C.—Killed: Sergeant Henry Sullivan; Private Tim. Purcell.

Company D.—Killed: Privates L. R. Smith and Joseph A. Frith. Wounded: Captain George F. Norton; Lieutenants W. H. Keiningham and A. Blair; Privates F. W. Gianini, H. W. Furcron, T. S. Morton, N. F. Wheat.

Company G.—Killed: Privates M. R. Mahone, C. C. Taliaferro, Robert F. Tyree.   Wounded: Lieutenant Eldridge Morris, Lieutenant L. R. Shell; Corporal Thomas H. Gunn; Privates J. R. Atkinson, Richard Jordan, Henry Brimmer; Sergeant George W. Ball.

Company H.—Killed: Sergeant Charles R. New; Private William M. Jackson.   Wounded: Lieutenant P. C. Cabell; Corporals Richard Chaddick and James A. Via; Private J. J. Chaddick.

Company I.—Killed: Privates H. Brooks, A. A. Burgess, R. L. Tabb, R. J. Moss   Wounded: Lieutenant B. F. Howard; Sergeants W. T. White and E. C. Goodson; Privates Paul McGrail, A. Rudd, A. Figner, James Ainsko, E. Taliaferro.

Company K.—Wounded: Corporal A. Weidenhahn.

Killed, 15; wounded, 39—54.

After this battle the regiment was disorganized, or, more properly stated, suspended.   The men having gone to their homes in Richmond, Companies K and E, whose time had expired, had left the regiment, Colonel Williams was a prisoner, and things looked very much like a close of the record and history of the Old First Virginia regiment; but about the 9th of June Captain J. W. Tabb, of Company I, took charge of the remains of the regiment, and procured a store on Cary, near Thirteenth street, as headquarters of the regiment.   He managed to get about forty-five of the men together.   On the 26th of June the regiment was again reported ready for duty, and the forty-five men, under the command of Captain G. F. Norton, of our Company, "D," joined the brigade on its way to Mechanicsville.   Halted during the night near the bridge over the Chickahominy.   Crossed that river on the morning of the 27th, and were posted as reserve in rear of Gaines's Mill while that battle was being fought.   The 28th and 29th was passed in following up the enemy on his retreat to James river.   Early on the 30th crossed the Chickahominy and participated in the battle of Frazier's Farm, losing the following men:

Company B.—Wounded: Lieutenant L. S. Robins; Sergeants J. L. Littlepage and J. Q. Figg.

Company D.—M. J. Wingfield was taken prisoner.   He sat down on the captured cannon and lit his pipe, when the enemy charged and retook the guns and captured him.

Company K.—Corporal A. Weidenhahn, wounded and left in the enemy's hands; our Chaplain, the Rev. Mr. Martin, was also taken prisoner.

On the next day skirmishing was going on in front all day. July 1st the battle of Malvern Hill was fought, but our services were not needed, we remaining in reserve.

A few days after the seven days' battles the regiment, which numbered now about thirty men, turned back towards Richmond, and went into camp near Darbytown. About the 1st of August Major W. H. Palmer, who had been ill from wounds received at the battle of Williamsburg, and typhoid fever contracted subsequently, took charge of the regiment and commenced to reorganize the same. In a short time we had 141 men in ranks.

On the morning of August 10th we left camp, marched to Richmond and took the cars for Gordonsville, where we landed the same evening. The next morning we marched towards Orange Courthouse, but after marching some distance under a broiling sun, we were ordered back. Passed through Gordonsville and went into camp near Mechanicsville, Louisa county, where we remained till the 16th, when we left, taking a northerly direction, marching on the Orange and Fredericksburg Turnpike, passing Orange Courthouse. On the 20th, crossed the Rapidan at Raccoon Ford. On the 21st, we were halted and held in reserve in the woods on the left of the road, about one-half mile south of Kelley's Ford. At that point, quite a brisk engagement was fought, cavalry and artillery being principally engaged. The enemey's shelling created a panic among the negro cooks, who, as they came running past our brigade, received the usual salutations, "Going all the way to-night, uncle? Anybody been troubling you? Hold on, you got plenty time; you are going the wrong way, you will get lost," &c. Most of them, however, had no time for talking, but one old fellow, less scared, or more tired, however, exclaimed : "I tell you, marsters, dem dar shells kept on singing 'whar you, nigger?' 'Whar you, nigger?' I tell you, when I heard dat, I got, I did."

While here, a Federal spy, neatly dressed in a new Confederate uniform, approached General Longstreet and presented to him a forged order from General Jackson, about the movement of his troops. General Longstreet, who knew all of Jackson's couriers, was not long in finding out who he had before him,

and in a few minutes the spy was swinging from a convenient
tree, and before life was hardly extinct his new boots were pulled
off by some enterprising Confed.

In the evening passed Stevensburg and marched to Brandy
Station, near the Rappahannock, halting on Mr. John Minor
Botts's farm. On the 23d, the battle of Rappahannock was
fought. It was principally an artillery engagement across the
river. On the 24th, marched up the Rappahannock, crossed the
Hazel river and halted near Jeffersonton; 25th, halted near
Waterloo Bridge; 26th, crossed the Rappahannock at Hinson's
Ford and reached Salem; 27th, arrived near White Plains, and
halted near Thoroughfare Gap. During the night the horses of
the officers stampeded, wounding two men; one of them, Thomas
Durham, of Company G, had his ear cut off. On perceiving his
wound, he clapped his hand to the wounded part and exclaimed,
" I have got a one 'ear turlough!" After the horses stampeded,
a big woodpile tumbled down, which, considering that the night
was pitch dark, did not help to make us very comfortable; 28th,
passed through the Gap, in which the enemy's dead were still
lying from the previous day's fight; passed through Haymarket
and Gainesville, halting about three miles from the latter place,
near Manassas.

This march to Manassas was peculiarly trying to the men,
sometimes marching all night, and receiving orders to move from
a place which we had not reached, when the orders to move were
received, then standing in the road waiting for the column to
move, besides having nothing to eat, except what we could find
in the fields – green corn and apples being principally our diet.
Often when some of the men left ranks to plunder an apple tree,
General Corse, in command of the brigade, would create a laugh
by calling out to them, " Come back here, you miserable stragglers, to desert your colors for a few green apples," but he was
paid back in the same coin, when he and his staff halted some-
where on the road to chat with the ladies, by the whole brigade
yelling at him, "Come back from there, you miserable straggler."

29th.—Heavy skirmishing going on all day in our front, and
subjected to shelling. On the 30th, the second battle of Manassas was fought.

Our brigade, under the command of Colonel Corse, of the
Seventeenth, (our brigade commander having been placed in

command of Longstreet's division, and having detached our Major, W. H. Palmer, as his Chief of Staff) was ordered to the right, and took our place in line of battle. About 4:30 o'clock P. M. the fight was in full blast. We were ordered to charge, and succeeded in driving the enemy from his line, near the Chinn House, capturing two batteries. Colonel F. G. Skinner, who led the regiment, here immortalized himself by riding into the enemy's artillery and cutting down the cannoniers far ahead of our charging line, but he was so badly wounded as to render him unable for field duty thereafter.

General M. D. Corse, commanding brigade, in his report published in the *Southern Historical Society Papers*, has the following :

Lieutenant-Colonel Skinner (First Virginia), dashing forward in advance of the whole line, was the first to reach the battery, and I saw him dealing deadly blows with his sabre to the Yankee gunners. The steady veteran, Terry, with the gallant Twenty-fourth, delivered a destructive volley into the enemy's ranks on our left, and pushed forward to the charge. The valiant Patton led the heroic Seventh Virginia. Its list of casualties in officers and men gives proof they were where the battle raged fiercely. Colonel Patton, Lieutenant-Colonel Floweree, Major Swindler and Adjutant Patton, all fell severely wounded in this brilliant onset. The ever-ready First, as usual, did its work manfully. Major Clements, with the war-worn Eleventh, moved forward with veteran firmness. The Seventeenth, led by the ardent Lieutenant-Colonel Marye, advanced in perfect line. Just before reaching the battery, Colonel Marye fell, wounded severely, and under command of the intrepid Major Herbert, the regiment continued the charge. The charge was a success; the enemy was driven from his guns, his infantry supports scattered, and his battery taken.

CASUALTIES IN THE BRIGADE.

	KILLED.	WOUNDED.	MISSING.	TOTAL.
First Virginia regiment,	4	26	1	31
Seventeenth Virginia regiment,	4	44	...	48
Eleventh Virginia regiment,	9	55	...	64
Seventh Virginia regiment,	5	48		53
Twenty-fourth Virginia reg't,	11	67	...	78
	33	240	1	274

The following is a list of casualties in the regiment. Those marked " killed " include all that died from wounds :

Field and Staff.—Wounded: Lieutenant-Colonel Fred. G. Skinner.

Company B.—Killed: Corporal Gus G. Goddin; Privates C. C. Carter, John W. Ratcliffe, J. T. Shiflett. Wounded: Sergeants Benjamin M. Crow, L. W. Ogden; Privates William A. Mallory, Richard H. Street. Prisoner: Sergeant J. L. Littlepage,

Company C.—Killed: Lieutenant John H. Donahoe.

Company D.—Killed: Sergeant W. A. Morris. Wounded: Lieutenant E. P. Reeve; Privates G. L. Meenley, T. S. Morton, I. T. Porter, L. R. Wingfield, A. G. Steger, J. E. Dooley. Prisoner: Private H. M. Walthall.

Company G.—Wounded: Private Robert G. Stewart.

Company H.—Killed: Captain W. E. Tysinger; Private W. M. Wight. Wounded: Sergeant John W. Wynne; Privates John A. Meanley, —— Nuckols.

Company I.—Killed: Captain J. W. Tabb; Privates James Ainsko and Jacob H. Smith. Wounded: Lieutenant H. C. Ballou; Corporal C. L. Parker; Privates J. T. Ayres, G. R. Glinn.

Killed and died from wounds, 11; wounded, 20; prisoners, 2—33.

Pollard's Southern History of the War, Volume I, page 462, contains the following:

"The First Virginia, which opened the fight on the 18th of July, 1861, with over 600, now reduced to less than eighty members, is winning new laurels; but out of the little handful more than a third have already bit the dust."

Early the next morning we crossed the battlefield, where thousands of dead and wounded lay in the broiling sun. They must have suffered fearfully; but such is war. The battle was fought nearly over the same ground occupied by the battle of July 21, 1861, with this singular difference: that our troops occupied nearly the same position the Federals held in '61.

We crossed Bull Run at Sudley's Ford September 1st, passed Chantilly and halted near Germantown. Here Jackson was engaged in battle during that day. Our brigade, under command of Colonel Corse, was sent into the woods on the right of the road during the night, and after marching and counter-marching all night, formed in line of battle; when day came we were facing our own wagon train.   On the 2d, marched *via* Dranesville to Leesburg.   3d. Halted near White's Ford, on the Potomac.   Here all the sick and barefooted men in the army were sent to Winchester, while we received three days' rations. 5th. Marched through Leesburg and crossed the Potomac into Maryland, halting near Buckstown on the 6th, reaching Frederick Junction, near the Monocacy railroad bridge, on the 7th.   This bridge was blown up the next day.   We stopped here for three days, having a good time bathing in the river, and getting something better to eat than raw corn and green apples.

On the 10th, we passed through Frederick City, Middletown and Boonsboro, on the turnpike, and reached Hagerstown on the evening of the next day.

On the 14th, ordered to Boonsboro to support General D. H. Hill's division, which held the gap at South Mountain.   Arrived there late in the evening, when we were placed in position on the hill to the left of the turnpike, where we engaged the enemy. While marching in column of fours, a spent six-pound shot struck J. H. Daniel, of Company " H," on the rump, and knocked him about ten feet without seriously injuring him.   Our loss was as follows:

Wounded: Lieutenant W. H. Keiningham, Company D; Privates J. H. Daniel, W. H. Smith, and W. P. Pumphrey of Company H.   The latter was left in the enemy's hands.

A. Jeff. Vaughan, Company G, was captured.

During the night we fell back, crossed Antietam Creek, and halted in line of battle on the south of Sharpsburg.   The battle of Sharpsburg commenced on the 16th, but we were not engaged till the 17th, when we were attacked by the enemy (Burnside's corps).   Not being strong enough to hold our position, we were forced to fall back; but just then, General A. P. Hill's corps came up, and the enemy was driven back to where he started. Private W. J. Mallory, Company B, was wounded.

18th.—Skirmishing all day.   At night, about 11 P. M., left Sharpsburg and crossed the Potomac near Shepherdstown.

Just before leaving Sharpsburg, Captain George F. Norton detailed Corporal L. Carral, with six men, to fill the canteens with water.   On his way to the water, he observed a warehouse where whiskey was stored, in charge of a guard from a Georgia regiment. He marched his detail up, relieved the Georgia guard, and instead of bringing the canteens back with water, filled them with whiskey, which caused the step of most of the men to be rather uncertain in fording the stream.

On the 19th, halted near Shepherdstown. On the 20th, marched to the Valley turnpike and halted near Martinsburg, by a big spring, where we encamped till the 27th. Most of our men were shoeless and deficient in clothing, and rest was much needed.

On the 27th we marched to within three miles of Winchester, and camped at the Washington Spring for a month.

Here ended the campaign. The troops were often without rations; they were deficient in clothing, especially in shoes. Walking barefooted over the rocky roads was more than most of us were used to. It was a painful sight to see the bloody and blistered feet as the men moved wearily along, but however much they suffered, they managed to keep up.

A great many recruits were sent to our regiment while here, but among them were few that came from Richmond. There the regiment was in bad repute; it was considered "an unlucky regiment." We again numbered over 200 men present. Among the recruits was one little fellow from Chesterfield, named Hancock, not much over four feet high. Unable to carry a musket, the boys came to the conclusion he would not do, and told him to go to Dr. Redford, (our acting Commissary Sergeant, Ellis Redford,) who, after stripping him and sounding his lungs in a professional way, pronounced him "unfit for duty," and gave him a certificate, written with charcoal on a piece of newspaper, to that effect. Little Hancock, highly elated, carried this to the Colonel, who laughed and forwarded him to the Brigade Surgeon. The consequence of the joke was, he got off with a long furlough. Here, also, Colonel L. B. Williams, who had been badly wounded and left a prisoner at Williamsburg, joined the regiment and took command, but we lost our Major, W. H. Palmer, who was transferred to A. P. Hill's command, as Chief of Staff.

October 31st we left our camp near Winchester, passed through Front Royal, crossing the Blue Ridge Mountains, and after three days' hard marching, arrived at Culpeper Courthouse November 2d, where we went into camp.

About the 1st of December, we left Culpeper Courthouse, and after several days' marching over muddy roads, arrived in the vicinity of Fredericksburg.

On the 10th of December the enemy crossed the river on pontoons below Fredericksburg, and we were placed in the line of works, holding a position about the centre of our line. While here old Major Dooley, and his friend John Mitchell, paid us a visit and took a look at the situation.

On the 13th we were placed in rear as reserve on a high hill overlooking the river and valley below, on which the battle was in full progress. It was a magnificent sight to see those lines in blue advance to the attack only to be driven back in confusion, and hear the music of the wild Confederate yell. But our stay was of short duration. Orders came for the brigade to support the troops in front of Marye's Hill on our left, but these men managed to sustain themselves, though sorely pressed.

On our way from the works General Kemper addressed the regiment in the following words: "Men of the First Virginia regiment—you who have on so many hard fought fields gained the name of the 'Bloody First'—to-day your country calls on you again to stand between her and her enemy, and I know you will do your duty."

The men responded with one of those yells that could be heard for miles.

We relieved the troops about 4 P. M. While in reserve the regiment lost three men wounded: Sergeant W. H. Dean and Privates W. L. Spraggins, of Company G, and John Moriarty, of Company C. The regiment was then posted in the sunken road below and in front of Marye's Hill, for which a hot contest had raged all day. The enemy's dead and wounded lay in heaps in our front; some within ten feet, and the groaning and praying of the wounded men was fearful to hear. The horrors of this night were still more vividly brought before us by the appearance of an *Aurora Borealis*, or northern light, which for a time illuminated the heavens and exposed to our view the suffering wounded lying in front of us. The musketry firing was kept up at intervals during the night, rendering it well nigh impracticable for either side to help them. Some of our men, however, did get some shoes from the dead, which was excusable, as we were badly shod. Several of the enemy's officers and men came into our lines, and were dispatched to the rear. They mistook their

way, which was natural enough during the night.   In the morning the enemy made another attempt to charge this position, but
soon abandoned the task as useless, and the balance of the day
was spent in skirmish firing.   At night the enemy recrossed the
river, and the morning of the 15th found nothing for us to do but
to go back to our camp.

On the 25th we moved camp to within two miles of Guinea's
Station, where we erected our winter quarters and made our-
selves comfortable.   An occasion to be remembered was the
Christmas dinner furnished us by the ladies of Richmond.
During this time several big snow-ball battles took place, in
some of which there were over 20,000 men engaged.

February 13th, 1863, left camp and marched to line of works
above Fredericksburg.   Worked one day to strengthen the line
near the Rappahannock river.   The next day were ordered to
follow the brigade on its way to Richmond, and overtook them
at Hanover Junction.   After two days of miserable marching, on
account of the bad weather and roads, halted a few hours to rest
at Hanover Junction; then set off in a tremendous snow storm
towards Richmond.   Camped that night near the head of the
Richmond and County road.   The next day we passed through
Richmond and camped near Manchester, on the Richmond and
Petersburg Turnpike, and on the following day reached Chester
Station, where we camped until March 1st.   While here we had
a big snow-ball battle with Jenkins's South Carolina brigade.

On March 1st we marched to Petersburg, passing through that
city, and halted to camp near Prince George Courthouse, and
commenced regular camp duty, drilling, &c.   On the 15th the
regiment was sent to Fort Powhatan.   Marched seventeen miles
and camped for the night; resumed the march next morning and
arrived at the fort at 10 A. M., where we remained strengthening
the works until the 19th.   A fearful snow storm set in, on account
of which work was suspended.   That evening received orders to
return to camp; marched five miles, and halted for the night in a
deserted farm house.   On the 20th, at daybreak, resumed march,
and reached camp at 1 P. M.   The snow was eighteen inches
deep.   At 3 P. M. struck tents, and marched to Petersburg and
quartered in a large warehouse during that night.

March 21st, at 10 A. M., took the cars for Goldsboro', N. C.

Arrived there on the night of 22d, and camped near that town until the next day, when the cars took us to Kinston, where we arrived that evening and went into camp south of the Neuse river, resuming drilling and other camp duty. 29th. Started on a scout with Seventh Virginia regiment, under command of Colonel Williams, towards Newberne; marching and counter-marching for two days through the swamps, and returned to camp after a slight skirmish near Tuscarora, on the railroad.

April 4th, received marching orders. Recrossed the Neuse river and camped at the depot in Kinston, waiting for transportation. Took the cars early on the 5th, passing Goldsboro' and Weldon. We halted at Franklin Station, on the Blackwater river, where we went into regular camp until the 11th, when we commenced our march under Longstreet to Suffolk, near which place we arrived on the 13th; formed in line of battle and entrenched ourselves, doing picket duty. Remained here until the 3d of May, when at 3 P. M. we started on a retrograde movement for Blackwater river, marching all night; crossed the river at South Quay at 10 A. M. on the next day, being a march of thirty-two miles, which nearly broke the men down. The full moon was shining brightly during the night's march, and the road on which we were marching ran nearly all the way through swamps, filled with the biggest kind of frogs, who appeared to have gotten up a special concert for us. The noise they succeeded in producing was simply immense, but far from agreeable to us as we wearily passed along.

Rested here till the morning of the 5th, when we reached Jerusalem, after marching twelve miles. Made seventeen miles on the 6th, and camped at Littleton for the night. On the 7th made twenty-two miles, and were placed on picket duty during the night, expecting a cavalry attack. On the 8th, made within six miles of Petersburg, and halted for the night.

On the 9th we passed through Petersburg and halted for the night on Dunlop's farm. The next day we reached Falling Creek, near Chester Station, and camped there a few days. Then started again, marched through Richmond and halted at Taylorsville the following day, where we went into camp.

On June 3d started again—towards Tappahannock this time; made twenty-one miles and halted for the night in Caroline county. On the next day marched seventeen miles and camped in King & Queen county. On the 5th passed through Newtown and halted that night half a mile beyond that village.

In passing through Newtown—this being the whole of Pickett's division—we heard some of the country people exclaim, " I never knew there were so many men in the world!" On the following day, no enemy appearing, we were ordered back to camp, which we reached on the night of the 7th. The next day, the 8th, we started again; leaving Taylorsville, marched through Caroline, Spotsylvania and Orange counties (passing near Orange Courthouse), we arrived at Culpeper Courthouse, where we remained three days. 14th. Ordered to prepare for light marching order, and three days' rations were issued. Started in the direction of Winchester, passed through Culpeper, and camped for the night near our old camp ground, two miles west of the town. 15th. Made eighteen miles, and halted at Gaines' Cross Roads. 16th. Passed Markham Station and halted at Paris for two days; then marched *via* Upperville, over the Blue Ridge Mountains, through Snickersville Gap to Snickersville.

On the 20th we crossed the Shenandoah river at Snicker's Ferry. The stream was very rapid and the water reached up to our armpits. Camped at night near Berryville, Clarke county. Clothing was issued to the men while here. Camped here until the 23d, when we passed through Berryville and reached Darksville. 24th. Passed Martinsburg and reached Williamsport, Maryland, at which point we had to ford the Potomac River, and halted for the night. On the 25th halted one mile beyond the town. 26th. Resumed march, passed through Hagerstown, Middletown, Marion, up the Cumberland Valley and bivouaced at Greencastle, Pennsylvania. 27th. Passed through Greencastle and Chambersburg, and halted to camp three miles beyond the last named town, on the York Road. Rested here one day. At 4 A. M. on the 29th, marched back through Chambersburg and halted in a large barn about a mile south of the town, on the road to Greencastle, where we did picket duty.

Chambersburg had the appearance of a deserted village on a wet Sunday. All the liquor had been placed in the court-house, and was under guard. The few people we saw had no great friendship to bestow on us " Rebels," but the farmers outside the town took things more pleasantly, and we got along very agreeably with them.

On the morning of the 2d July, our division (Pickett's) started, at 2 o'clock, on the Gettysburg Road. We pushed on as fast as possible, crossing the South Mountain, and made about twenty-three miles by 2 o'clock P. M , when we halted about three miles from Gettysburg. The battle was in full progress when we arrived, and the men were all anxious to go in, but word came we were not needed then. A little before daybreak the morning of the 3d, we moved to the right and were placed in line of battle in rear of Cemetery Ridge.

About 1 o'clock P. M. our artillery commenced the "ball," the whole line firing at once. A few minutes elapsed, and the fiery messengers of the enemy made their appearance in return. Thunder answered thunder, and the very ground appeared to tremble. Three hundred cannon were doing their best to match the very elements of heaven. Fifteen men of my company ("D") were now detailed as skirmishers and crawled to the top of the hill; meanwhile, the shells fell thickly in the line of battle, and the regiment suffered severely. After the artillery duel had lasted about two hours we were ordered to charge. The line of skirmishers advanced, and the line of battle followed about 200 yards in the rear. In front of the enemy's position was a deep ravine, through which our line could not well charge; they had, therefore, to go to the left, and "left oblique," was the command given to the main line, while the skirmishers advanced to the edge of the ravine. All during this time the line was exposed to a terrible fire, but the line would close up as the men fell. Forward we swept on until the first line was taken. The guns are ours, over 500 prisoners are taken; but the fire does not slacken, and our men are getting fewer and fewer. The reinforcement has not dared to enter this death-trap, and "Pickett's Division," or all that was left of it, being about one tenth, slowly retires to the point from whence it issued, "to do or die." The skirmishers were also preparing to retire, when Wilcox's brigade (which had remained in reserve up to this time near the place from where we started) came rushing down among our skirmish line. Being, however, unable to accomplish anything, and subjected to the enemy's fire, now concentrated on them, they soon retired, mingling with our skirmishers, and the awful list of casualties was still further increased by this movement. Thirteen colors are lying among the dead and dying, ours among them. The color guard is dead and the color sergeant has lost his arm; our Colonel lay dying on the field; twenty-three men are killed from the regiment, and nearly 100 more are left on the field wounded and missing. The regiment lost about 120 men out of about 160 who went into that charge.

The accompanying list of the casualties is nearly correct:

Field and Staff.—Killed: Colonel L. B. Williams. Wounded: Major F. H. Langley; Sergeant-Major J. R. Polack; Color-Sergeant William M. Lawson.*

Company B.—Killed: Private Fendal Franklin. Wounded: Captain T. H. Davis;* Lieutenant J. A. Payne; Corporal W. J. Carter;* Privates George R. Heath,* James Stagg,* Joseph Daniel,* H. L. Speckard, R. H. Street, W. J. Mallory.*

Company C.—Killed: Captain James Holloran. Wounded: Lieutenant John E. Dooley.*

Company D.—Killed: Privates Willie Mitchell, D. S. Edwards, M. J. Wingfield, J. W. Freeman. Wounded: Captain G. F. Norton; Lieutenants E. P. Reeve, W. H. Keiningham,* and A. Blair; Sergeant J. M. Finn;* Corporal G. E. Craig; Privates J. B. Angle, W. J. Armstrong, J. F. Wheeley, G. W. Johnson,* J. C. Keiningham,* T. S. Morton,* E. Priddy, S. L. Wingfield, L. R. Wingfield,* C. M. Sublett. Prisoners: Sergeant J. H. Kepler; Private N. W. Bowe.

Company G.—Killed: Private William F. Miller. Wounded: Captain E. Morris; Lieutenant W. T. Woody; Sergeant Thomas W. Hay;* Corporal John Allen; Privates Thomas H. Durham,* James Farrar, H. C. Fergusson,* C. W. Gentry, B. H. Hord,* W. T. Kendrick, C. A. Redford, T. S. Rogers, A. Jeff Vaughan, Robert R. Walthall. Prisoners: Sergeant George W. Ball; Privates B. F. Ashby, A. Haskins.

Company H.—Killed: Sergeant C. P. Hansford; Corporal Richard Chaddick; Privates W. J. Vaughan, Flowers, Nuckols, St. Clair, J. W. Paine, M. Brestrahan, W. S. Waddell. Wounded: Captain A. J. Watkins; Lieutenants E. W. Martin, P. C. Cabell; Sergeants T. R. Martin, R. H. Norvell; Privates W. B. Mosby,*

---

*Wounded left in enemy's hands—34.

3

J. H. Daniel, W. H. Denerson,* W. H. Anderson,* Sol. Banks,* R. E. Dignum,* F. Farson,* E. Fizer,* W. R. Kilby,* Thomas Mauring, J. J. Sinnott,* F. Smith, W. C. Hite.*   Prisoners: Privates Mat. Lloyd, Robert Lloyd.

Company I.—Killed: Lieutenant W. A. Caho; Corporal L. O. Eliett; Privates E. J. Griffin, Edwin Taliaferro, H. McLaughlan.   Wounded: Sergeant W. F. Terry; Corporals C. L. Parker,* J. T. Ayres,* T. E. Traylor; Privates R. O. Meredith,* G. W. Shumaker,* S. S. Neal,* C. A. Wills,* C. H. Chappell.   Prisoners: Sergeants John T. Crew, E. C. Goodson, W. T. White; Privates S. Clarke, W. C. Taliaferro.

Killed, 22; wounded, 71; prisoners, 12.

After the battle the survivors of Pickett's men, about 300, were gathered near the place from where they set out to make the deadly charge.   General Pickett came riding among them, and one long fellow from the Twenty-fourth Virginia regiment (Charlie Belcher by name) who had one of the two colors left to the division, called out to General Pickett: "General, let us go it again."   Just about this time General Kemper was carried by badly wounded—mortally, we thought—and General Pickett could not restrain his tears.   All at once General Lee and staff rode up, and taking General Pickett by the hand, General Lee remarked (I heard these words myself): "General, your men have done all that men could do, the fault is entirely my own."   The men were told they might go to their wagon train, where most of them spent the night.   The next morning when the regiment was called together it mustered about twenty-five men, under command of Captain B. F. Howard, Company I.   Sergeant-Major J. R. Polack, who had his left arm in a sling and his somewhat prominent nose damaged from the attention of the enemy on the previous day, procured a set of colors and commenced to waive them; but the boys, not seeing any fun in the movement, told him they declined to play color guard, and induced him to cease his demonstrations.

These colors had belonged to Holcombe's Legion, and were abandoned by them when they were retreating through our advancing ranks at the second battle of Manassas.

---

* Wounded left in enemy's hands—34.

We were now informed that Pickett's division was detailed as Provost Guard. Shortly afterwards about 4,000 prisoners were turned over to us, and in the evening we marched with them to Fairfield, where we halted for the night.

On the 5th we started early in the morning and entered the mountains. In the evening, firing could be heard in our rear, and as night drew near there was also the reports of musketry in our front. The prisoners appeared to be overjoyed, feeling certain that they would be set free, and our whole army would be captured; but the musketry in our front proved to be not the enemy, but our own men resting in the woods, cleaning their guns and shooting the old charges off. We also rested here on the mountain-top, near the Maryland line, till 2 A. M. on the 7th, when we started again, marching all that night, which was somewhat enlivened by the happy voice of "Bill" Deane, of Company G, whose gay tunes were thankfully accepted by friend and foe. The prisoners suffered very much for want of food. We did all that was in our power to relieve them, but there was not much to be had in the eating line until we reached Williamsport, which we did about 1 o'clock P. M. on the 8th. While passing Hagerstown that morning, several hundred more prisoners were added to the overcrowded ranks. These had been captured near Hagerstown from the enemy's cavalry on the previous day in an unsuccessful charge on our wagon train, at that point. On the 9th, the prisoners were turned over to General Imboden's command. On the 11th, the brigade re-crossed the Potomac, and was placed on picket duty south of the river guarding the roads. Remained there till the 13th, when the division crossed the Potomac, which we rejoined on the march to Martinsburg at 4 P. M. Marched under a heavy rain storm in total darkness until 2 A. M. on the 14th, passing through Martinsburg and halted in an open field one mile south of the town soaking wet, and without fire to dry ourselves. At 6 P. M. moved near the woods, and soon had large fires going.

15th.—Marched to Bunker Hill, seven miles, and remained there until the 19th, when we started again and camped at Smithfield for the night.

20th.—Left at daybreak, passed through Berryville and halted to camp near Millwood late that evening. At night the brigade was placed on outpost duty at Berry's Ferry. On the next morning, at 4 A. M., we were relieved and marched for Front Royal. Arrived at the Shenandoah river that evening, and forded it. The water being very swift and strong, we had hard work to get across. Passed Front Royal and camped for the night on the summit of the Blue Ridge, at Chester Gap, then partially in possession of the enemy's cavalry, but Corse's brigade had succeeded just in time in dislodging them the previous day by a sharp skirmish from taking possession of the main gap. On the 22d the brigade took position in line on the left; drove the enemy from the road, advanced down the mountain, scoured the country for several miles, driving the enemy from the road; resumed march for Culpeper, marching all that night knee deep in mud; reached Gaines's Cross-Roads early on the 23d, and rested for the day. 24th. Marched towards Culpeper Courthouse, which we reached on the 25th, and camped near it until August 3d, when we marched to the Rapidan river and halted near Mountain Run that night, where we went into regular camp, resuming drill, &c. By the return of the wounded, paroled prisoners, and recruits our regiment now numbered about 150 men.

By the death of Colonel L. B. Williams, who fell at Gettysburg, Major F. H. Langley was promoted to Lieutenant-Colonel, and Captain George F. Norton was made Major. There was no further change of regimental officers during the war.

September 9th. Brigade was ordered to Richmond. Marched by the way of Louisa Courthouse, over the Mountain Road to Richmond; thence to Chaffin's farm, where we arrived on the 13th. Here we halted in the winter quarters put up by General Wise's men, until the 25th, when we marched back to Richmond and took the cars of the Richmond, Fredericksburg and Potomac Railroad for Taylorsville, where we arrived about the middle of the night. Here we built our log cabins and went into winter quarters, guarding the roads and bridges in the neighborhood. While here received overcoats and supply of clothing, donated by the City Council of Richmond. Here we spent a very pleasant time, as going to Richmond, or giving a grand ball at Ashland, only a few miles off, was a frequent occurrence.

January 8th, 1864. Received marching orders, embarked on cars and halted at Richmond at 2 o'clock on the following morning, and marched over the deserted streets covered with snow, to the Petersburg depot, where the brigade took the cars for Petersburg, at which place we halted, near the reservoir, to cook rations, after which we marched to the depot and took the cars for Weldon, North Carolina, where we arrived on the next morning.   Remained here two days awaiting transportation, then took the cars and halted at Goldsboro', where we went into camp two miles west of the town, near the railroad, until the 29th, when we were sent to Kinston to join Pickett's expedition.

On the 30th of January commenced the march to Newberne; halted six miles from Trenton that night, crossed the Trent river the next day, passing through swamps most of the way, and camped within ten miles of Newberne for the night.   The next day, February 1st, we arrived within three miles of Newberne, in front of the enemy's lines, where we halted in line of battle on the south side of the Trent river.   Our force consisted of our (Terry's) brigade and Barton's brigade.   Our company was detailed for picket duty, and posted on the bank of the river, after a night's march through the tall broom-straw, without knowing where we were going or what was in our front.   The next day, in the evening, after kindling fires on the whole line, we fell back, marching all night over roads badly cut up and very swampy.   Halted near the crossing of the Trent river, and arrived again at Kinston on the following day.

The force engaged under Pickett succeeded in capturing about 500 prisoners and a section of artillery, which was turned over to the Fayette Artillery.   Among the prisoners were many North Carolina deserters, several of whom were afterwards hung, by General Pickett's orders, at Kinston.

On the 5th we marched to Goldsboro', which we reached on the 7th, and went into camp near that town.   On the 18th a man from the 7th Virginia was shot for deserting.   It was a solemn occasion, the first that ever took place in our brigade. The brigade was drawn up on three sides of a square; facing on the fourth side was the doomed man, pinioned, blindfolded and bound to a stake.   In the centre stood the firing party, a detail of two men from each company of the regiment to which the deserter belonged, in two ranks and about twenty or thirty feet from the command.   Half the muskets only were loaded with ball cartridge, so that no one who fired knew who fired the fatal shots.   The band played a dead march, the chaplain spoke a few final words with the condemned, stepped aside, and at the command the fire was delivered. The unfortunate man was riddled by half a dozen bullets; when the smoke cleared away he was hanging a helpless mass on the stake.

On the 20th we started again for Kinston, where we arrived on the 22d, and halted to camp on the north of the town, on the Washington farm. On the 28th moved camp to the south side of Neuse river. On the 4th of March we took the cars for Wilmington, North Carolina; passing Goldsboro', arrived at Wilmington the evening of the next day.

On the 6th the brigade marched through the sandy streets of Wilmington for the wharf, where we embarked on board of an English steamer (a blockade runner), which carried us to Smithville, a town located at the mouth of the Cape Fear river, and went into camp about a mile south of the town. On the 17th the brigade was inspected by General Herbert, who commanded the post. Our camp being close to the ocean shore, we could watch the enemy's war ships as they pursued our blockade runners, sometimes coming within reach of our batteries, which would open on them. During one of these engagements one of the enemy's steamers was sunk by a shell from a Whitworth gun. We lived mostly on oysters and crabs, and most of us would have been satisfied to remain at this point for the rest of the war. While here the Twenty-fourth regiment having, it was said, become too fond of the farmers' pigs, was sent to Fort Caswell to reinforce the garrison there, where it remained until the brigade returned from the "seaside resort." It was this regiment that prevented the capture of one of our blockade runners, which had run aground near Fort Caswell, by taking possession of the steamer and supporting the gun which drove the enemy's fleet off.

On March 24th our stay ended here; marched to the town and got on the steamer "Cape Fear," which took us, after a night's run, back to Wilmington, where we found two inches of snow on the ground; thence by rail to Goldsboro', which we reached the same day, and halted at our old camp till April 1st, when we started on the march for Tarboro', which we reached after a three days' march. Crossed the Tar river and camped one and a half miles on the eastern bank of that river. On the 15th General Hoke took command of the force, which consisted of our (Terry's), Ransom's and Hoke's brigades, Thirty-eighth Virginia battalion of artillery, and Dearing's cavalry, and we started for Plymouth. Arrived in front of that town after two and a half days' marching. On the evening of the 17th deployed as skirmishers in front of Fort Gray, the left of the line resting on the river. In the evening our artillery and skirmish line opened on a passing gunboat, which was badly damaged. A detachment of our regiment took position on the river at an old frame house, which its occupants had apparently just left. During the night the house was found to contain eggs, butter, flour, and other good things, and our men went to work to have a feast, lighting the fires and making a big light. The window facing our artillery was pretty soon saluted by our shells, the house being taken for one of the enemy's gun-boats. On sending word to our guns the fire ceased, happily without injury to any one, and the men completed their cooking operations. The next morning this house became a regular target for the guns at Fort Gray, and after a few shots the house was totally ruined and one of our company (Delaware McMinn) was killed, and several wounded, after which the rest of us made our way back to the regiment.

On the next day, in the evening, we were sent around to the right, marching about six miles, and halted in front of Fort Wessells, located one thousand yards from the town, and commanding the main road. Arriving after dark, we were placed in position to support Hoke's brigade, which commenced an unsuccessful charge on the fort, the defences of the fort being of such nature that it was impossible for the men to get in it. The enemy used hand grenades, together with the firing, to which the gunboats added with their big shells, making streaks of fire through the air, produced a beautiful illumination to view. Hoke's brigade being withdrawn, our brigade was deployed in a skirmish line encircling the fort; after which, General Dearing placed the Fayette Artillery in position close to the stubborn fort, and the artillery boys did their duty well. Their shells completely raked the whole top of the fort off, and the garrison was glad to surrender after being subjected to this terrible fire for about half an hour. During all this time the huge shells of the gunboats were flying about us; one of the caissons of the Fayette Artillery was blown up, but the brigade came out without loss. The 19th was passed in reserve, skirmishing going on in our front, by which one of our men was killed. During that night our iron-clad ram, Albemarle, arrived, and passing the forts, cleaned out the enemy's gunboats, sinking several, after which it turned its attention to the enemy in town. Early this morning our regiment was deployed as skirmishers in front of Fort Williams. Ransom's brigade succeeded in getting into town on the right of our line, and driving the enemy through the town, forced them to surrender to Hokes's men, which held the position on the left. Fort Williams, the centre of the defences, held out a little longer, but the contest soon became hopeless, the enemy's flag went down and the town was ours. About 10 A. M. we entered the town, stacked arms and helped ourselves to the good things stored therein, it being the depot for the enemy's supplies for the eastern part of North Carolina, who had no idea of our intended visit. We supplied ourselves with new rifled muskets, blankets and general outfit. Twenty-five cannons, several hundred horses and wagons, and a large supply of commissary stores were captured, also about sixteen hundred prisoners, consisting of the Eighty-fifth New York, One Hundred and Sixty-third Pennsylvania, Sixteenth Connecticut, a negro regiment, and a battalion of artillery, all under command of General Wessell, who was also captured.

It was quite amusing to see our men turning their war-bags (as they called the haversacks) inside out, dropping the old corn-dodgers and pieces of rancid bacon in the streets, to make room for cakes, preserves, pies and things, and going through the houses so lately occupied by the enemy's officers and families, but now all deserted, breaking the large mirrors to get a piece of looking-glass, pulling the strings out of elegant pianos to hang the cups on, and generally helping themselves to things that were useful or useless to them.

Our losses in the regiment during the three days were: Killed—Privates Delaware McMinn, of Company D, and M. Consadine, of Company C. Wounded—Lieutenant J. A. Payne, Company B; Privates T. J. Robertson, Company D; Wilson B. Joseph and J. Belcher, of Company H.

At night went into camp about a mile and a half south of the town.

On the 24th detailed to do guard duty in Plymouth. 25th. Rejoined the brigade and marched to Jamesville. On the 26th arrived near Washington, North Carolina. The next morning took position in line of battle to attack the works.   While here Lieutenant A. Blair, from our company, shot himself accidentally with a pistol, seriously wounding himself in the leg; no fight, however, took place, the enemy having left on our approach. The Third Virginia regiment was left here to garrison the forts, and only joined the brigade again in the following June. 28th. Reached Toronto creek, and the next day arrived at Greenville, where we halted until May 2d. Commenced the march for Newberne, passed through Greenville and moved southeast twenty-three miles.   3d. Crossed the Neuse river on pontoons twelve miles below Kinston and camped at night on the banks of the Trent river near Pollocksville.   The next day crossed the Trent river on pontoons, passed through Pollocksville and arrived before Newberne.

On the 5th formed line of battle on Colonel Hill's farm.   In the evening the regiment was thrown out as skirmishers, under Major Norton, and halted, where we had a good view of the town; remained on picket duty near the river till the night of the 6th.   Preparations were in full progress to make a general attack on the works, and already one of the forts, with sixty prisoners, were in our hands, when orders came to return to Kinston.

Our company being on picket, brought up the rear. Late in the evening, commenced the march, which lasted most all night, going through water and mud; it being pitch dark, the men kept shooting their guns off to see the way. Recrossed the Trent river and halted near Pollocksville. 7th. Marched about sixteen miles and halted near the Neuse river, about twelve miles from Kinston, where we crossed on the 3d.   The 8th, reached Kinston and halted near the bridge until the next day, when we took the cars, passed Goldsboro', and traveling all night reached Jarratt's Station during the morning of the 10th; found the bridge destroyed, it having been burned by the enemy on the 8th instant; had to march eleven miles to Stony creek, where we again took the cars, which landed us in Petersburg.

On our march through the city, we halted to receive a kind welcome by the ladies of Petersburg, who fed us on the best they could bring together; their treat was thankfully received.

Our brigade coming at this time to Petersburg, when Butler, with 30,000 men, was knocking at its gates, and the defenders too few for resistance, caused a feeling of general relief among the people. After a short halt we stopped for the night south of the town.

On the 11th we left our position near Swift creek, and after passing a large force of the enemy we formed in line of battle near Port Walthall Junction. On the 12th, marched to Half-Way house on the turnpike, and halted there in close column. Formed line of battle during a heavy shower of rain. In the evening, moved to the outer line of works near the railroad, and later at night marched to Drewry's Bluff, from which we moved to the Broad Rock race course, near Manchester, where we halted in line of breastworks expecting the enemy; this, however, turned out to be a false alarm, caused by the Militia cavalry from Richmond, who mistook for the enemy some men from our company who were on a scout. Halted here till 12 o'clock on the 14th, when we started for the front. Took position near Rice's Station, between the railroad and the turnpike, in breastworks. Fighting was going on on our left, where the enemy made several unsuccessful attacks on our works. On the 15th, at 7 P. M., we moved close to Drewry's Bluff, and halted in a piece of woods on the left of the Stage road.

About daybreak the column was in motion. Moving on the old Stage road (the extreme left of our line) we crossed Kingsland's creek and formed in line of battle in a narrow valley, shrouded in mist so dense that the eye could not pierce it, and we were only aware that it was filled with our friends preparing for the desperate struggle ahead by the clear and distinct words of commands from invisible officers marshalling an invisible host. The column was formed as follows: Gracie's Alabama brigade in front, our (Terry's or Kemper's) next, and Barton in the rear, Major Boggs's battery on the right. The position of the enemy was of great natural advantage, commanding an open field in front of several hundred yards in extent, strengthened by breastworks. Now the line was formed, and General Gracie's voice rang out, "Forward," and his men went ahead. Soon the scattering shots told of the skirmishers being busy, and then followed the charge, and the musketry mingled with the reports of Boggs's artillery; but when the Alabama brigade reached the front of the enemy's works they came to a halt in a creek or swamp. Our brigade had slowly been following them, the regiments moving in the following order: On the right was the Twenty-fourth, next the Eleventh, then ours (the First), and on the left was the Seventh. Gracie being unable to carry the works before him, called for support on Colonel R. L. Maury, of the Twenty-fourth, and that regiment came gallantly to his assistance; next the Eleventh went in, and then came our turn. We struck the point where the Stage road crosses the works, and passed without opposition. Marching about 100 yards down the road, we turned to the right towards the firing, and found ourselves in rear of the enemy's line. Coming across where their coffee was temptingly boiling, we stopped and helped ourselves to a good cup of coffee, which was a rare treat. After leaving the coffee-pots we struck a line of men on our right, who, after some talk, surrendered without firing, being completely taken by surprise. Meanwhile, the left of our regiment drew the attention of the enemy further to their front and lower down, who called out, "What regiment is that?" On receiving the answer, "the First Virginia," they turned on us with a volley at close range, which killed eight of our men. We then charged down among them, and those we found surrendered. The Seventh Virginia, which was ordered in after us, followed us, making a still greater curve around the enemy's rear, and came in on our left. General Heckman, who commanded the enemy's line at this point, rode up to them calling out, "Come on, boys; we are driving them back," mistaking them for his reinforcements. He was ordered to surrender; which he did, giving his sword to Colonel C. C. Floweree, of that regiment. Meanwhile, the Twenty-fourth and Eleventh Virginia regiments, which made the attack in front, had crossed, and assisted in the capture and defeat of the enemy. Barton's brigade, which then came up, was sent to the right, where the struggle was quite severe, especially with Corse's brigade whose loss was very heavy.

The loss by Heckman's brigade, consisting of the Ninth New Jersey, Twenty-third, Twenty-fifth and Twenty-seventh Massachusetts regiments alone, is stated by them as forty-two killed, 188 wounded, and 458 missing—together, 688. Our loss was also very heavy. The regiment lost ten killed and about twenty wounded.

The loss of our brigade, including the engagements until the 20th, are put down at 321, which includes a few missing, viz:

	KILLED.	WOUNDED.
First Virginia,	12	25
Seventh Virginia,	2	37
Eleventh Virginia,	15	94
Twenty-fourth Virginia,	28	108
	57	264

Our victory would have been complete if General Whiting, who had charge of the army at Petersburg, had but done his duty. By his failure to coöperate, we lost the opportunity to capture Butler's whole army, but the practical result was to relieve Richmond and Petersburg from imminent danger, and cause the enemy to retire to his base near Bermuda Hundreds.

The casualties of the regiment consisted of the following:

Company B.—Killed: Corporals W. A. Stoaber and Jerry Toomey; Private William H. Crigger. Wounded: Private William A. Mallory.

Company C.—Killed: Private Samuel Gillispie.

Company D.—Killed: Private Archie Govan. Wounded: Sergeant G. E. Craig; Private W. W. Turner. Prisoner: Private N. F. Wheat.

Company G —Killed: Private Robert R. Walthall. Wounded: Captain Eldridge Morris. Prisoner: Private A. Jeff. Vaughan.

Company H.—Killed: Sergeant John W. Wynne; Corporal J. A. Via. Wounded: Lieutenant W. E. Martin; Corporal R. N. Dunn; Private —— Morgan.

Company I.—Killed: Privates A. Figner and C. A. Wills. Wounded: Sergeant W. F. Terry; Privates R. A. Ashby, M. Hodges, and W. P. Smith.

Killed, ten; wounded, eleven; captured, two.

Those captured were carrying off prisoners, and mistook the road, instead of going to our rear, they went to the front.

After the battle we formed a line partly in the captured works and partly in new works erected by us, sending out our skirmishers well to the front, we halted here undisturbed the rest of the day and the following night. The next morning we followed the enemy towards the Howlett House and camped for the night at the Friends House.   On the 18th we were placed in a fort at the Howlett House, which was to be built so as to command the river at that point.   Two or three parties who were detailed for this purpose had been driven away by the enemy's gun-boats, when our regiment and the Seventh Virginia were called on for this duty. The parties which preceded us had gone to the point under cover of darkness, but we moved to occupy it in the light of day and in full view of the gunboats, which opened a terrific fire as we crossed an open field.   It was, however, not effective, as we rushed to the position in open order, every man on his own hook.   The enemy then ranged their gunboats in position and concentrated on us their fire for about eleven hours.   Every species of missile was hurled against us from eleven gunboats, while we were unable to respond with a single shot.   When we arrived in position the lines for the fort were nearly marked out.   We laid aside our arms, "spades being trumps," and in a short time had thrown out earth enough to afford us considerable protection. The enemy used some very heavy ordnance, which frequently buried the men so deep under the earth thrown in our trench by the explosions, as to render it difficult for the mass of tired men to rise out of it; but we held our position in spite of the enemy's utmost efforts to dislodge us.   Our losses were two killed and several wounded from the regiment.   Our loss was not as heavy as in many other actions in which we were engaged, but it was a trying time, peculiarly so, that we had to remain passive during all that time.   Darkness came and we left that awful pit looking like a set of miners returning from the bowels of the earth.

Our casualties were as follows :

Killed: Private J. R. Wesley; Corporal A. A. Chappell, Company I. Wounded (most of them stunned by concussion): Private E. Priddy, Company D; Sergeant R. E. Armstrong, Lieutenant P. C. Cabell, Company H; Captain B. F. Howard, Privates E. G. Loving, G. W. Bowler, A. T. Minor, Company I.

The following day we took position in line near the Clay House, and in the evening marched towards Richmond, which we reached on dawn of the 20th; marched through the streets, each regiment of the brigade bearing one of the captured flags taken

at Drewry's Bluff.   In the evening a part of the brigade, including
a portion of our regiment, got on board of a train and were sent
to Millford Station, where we arrived late that evening and halted
in the town for the night.   About 10 o'clock on the following day
the enemy's cavalry, Torbert's division, the advance guard of
Grant's army, appeared in sight, and we thinking them on a raid,
prepared to give them a warm reception.   The part of our regiment present, about sixty men, were distributed in and around
the buildings.   Major George F. Norton, the only field officer
present, took command, and J. R. Pollock, our Sergeant Major,
acted   as   Assistant   Adjutant-General   of   all   the   forces.   I
being   the   only   non-commissioned   officer   from   my   company
present, had charge of the company, consisting of ten men, and
posted them in a blacksmith shop.   The enemy noticing us,
halted a while, and then came charging down among us, but only
to be sent back from where he started.   This was repeated several times, when they gave it up, having lost several of their men
and horses.   They then dismounted, and being largely reinforced,
opened fire on us from their rifles and a battery they brought in
position.   Major Norton now sent the Eleventh Virginia forward
over the open field to charge, and they succeeded in driving the
enemy some distance, but as the enemy's force grew larger and
their lines swept around us from river to river, we were ordered
to retire, which we did, with some loss, principally among the
men of the Eleventh, its loss being about sixty, mostly captured.
This action, as we afterwards discovered, was the cause of delaying
the whole of Grant's army, and it was the advance of the great
Northern host moving by the left flank from Spotsylvania we
had struck.   The delay gave General Lee time to reach Hanover
Junction first and select his line.   Major Norton and his men
were highly complimented by General Lee for the valuable service rendered by this action.   After the fight we fell back in the
direction of Spotsylvania Courthouse about eight miles, when we
halted to rest.

The northern writers state that we were driven from rifle pits
and entrenchments; this is an error.   We had no protection but
the buildings, and there were no more entrenchments there then
than may be found to-day; but our resistance may well have
made them believe that they were charging fortifications.

During the night a part of Lee's army passed us coming from

Spotsylvania Courthouse. In the morning we fell in with the rear guard and marched to Hanover Junction, where we were welcomed by the rest of our brigade. On the 23d, marched to Andersonville during the night, and threw up a line of works during the following day in rear of A. P. Hill's corps with shelling in our front. Halted here till the 27th, when we left at 10 o'clock A. M., and made seventeen miles, during an all day rain, and camped near Atlee's Station. In the evening of the following day we passed the station and marched about twelve miles towards Hanovertown, and camped about three miles north of Mechanicsville. On the evening of the 30th we marched for the line of entrenchments near Cold Harbor, and at night the regiment was sent into the woods in front of our lines to feel the enemy's position. It was so dark that our line became mixed up with that of the enemy's, and a scene of confusion ensued, the men not knowing friend from foe. When we got out of the woods we noticed several Federals in our ranks, which we claimed as prisoners; they got there by mistaking our line for theirs. We met with no loss, and returned to the works. On the evening of the 31st we moved two miles to the right. The next day (June 1st) there was heavy fighting to our right; also on the 2d, when General Early had a fight in our front, driving the enemy some distance; the 3d, more skirmishing in front, and heavy fighting on the right—expected an attack; 5th, more fighting in Kershaw's and Hoke's front on the right. On the 7th General Early's command drove in the enemy's skirmish line, taking about 100 prisoners in our front. Our line of pickets then advanced beyond that held by the enemy prior to the fight. This was a great relief to our main line, which had been subjected to the fire of the enemy's sharpshooters. The pickets continued their firing, and there was plenty of target exercise; but these targets would shoot back, and there was usually a very lively time on the picket line. Being on that duty one day I counted no less than twelve bullets which struck the top log of my pit. One bullet happened to strike just as I was about to shoot, and the splinters of wood from the log it hit gave me a black eye for weeks after. Private H. C. Bowe, of Company D, was also wounded here. On the 12th we were subjected to an enfilading fire of artillery. The next morning (the 13th) we found the enemy had left our front and were moving towards the river. At 8 A. M. we started, marching in a parallel line with the enemy, passing over the old battle ground of Gaines's Mill; crossed the Chickahominy river over McClellan's bridge, near Seven Pines, and halted near the battlefield of Frazier's Farm. On the 15th, marched up the Darbytown road, and after a short march camped for the night. On the next morning (the 16th) we started at daybreak; marched to Chaffin's Bluff and crossed the James river on a pontoon bridge. Passing over the battleground of Drewry's Bluff we got on the Petersburg turnpike, and nearly reached Port Walthall Junction. When quietly marching along, the head of the column was suddenly fired into by the enemy, who had possession of the road. We (Pickett's division) were then formed in line of battle on the turnpike, and sending out our skirmishers commenced to drive the enemy, and at night succeeded in regaining our first line of works, which had been vacated that morning by our troops having been called off to meet Grant's army at Petersburg, leaving only one cavalry regiment, which was unable to hold the enemy in check. The next day commenced with heavy skirmish firing. One of our men (Nobles, of Company C), had the canteens of water he was carrying shot through, and mistaking the water running down his unmentionables for blood cried out for the ambulance to carry him off, which resulted in a good laugh on finding out how he was shot. About 4 o'clock P. M. we commenced a charge along the whole line, we charging near the Clay house, and the whole of our outer line was recovered; not, however, without some loss. The regiment's loss in wounded was as follows:

Corporal G. L. Meenley, Privates Thomas W. Taylor, E. Priddy, Company D; Private G. E. Redford, Company H; Privates J. K. Yancy and J. H. James, Company I.

It afterwards appeared that General Lee did not intend to carry on the attack to such an extent, and he had sent his aides to stop the charge, but he was well satisfied with the result. He wrote the following letter to General Anderson after the charge:

"*General*,—I take great pleasure in presenting to you my congratulation upon the conduct of the men of your corps. I believe that they will carry anything they are put against. We tried very hard to stop Pickett's men from capturing the breastworks of the enemy, but couldn't do it. I hope his loss has been small.

(Signed.)   R. E. LEE, *General*.

Official: G. M. SORREL, Lieutenant-Colonel,
                    Acting Adjutant-General.
For Major-General G. A. Pickett, Commanding Division."

After taking the works, there was some heavy skirmishing in the thick woods in front of our position done that night, and the next day. During the morning a charge was made by our skirmish line, in which J. C. Keiningham was taken prisoner.

About the middle of the day we moved to the right. On the 19th continued the movement to the right, and halted near Swift Creek. Same evening moved back to our position occupied in the morning, and relieved Davis's brigade, and remained here doing picket duty and fortifying till the 30th, when we moved about half a mile to the right. The regiment, during this time received a good many recruits; some of them made excellent soldiers, but many were of no use at all, and should not have been sent into the field. Some of them looked like they had been resurrected from the grave, after laying therein for twenty years or more.

On the 16th of August our regiment, together with the Eleventh and Nineteenth, under the command of Lieutenant-Colonel Langley, from our regiment, were ordered to the north of James river. Crossed at Drewry's Bluff and camped near Chaffin's farm that night. The next day moved along the line of works, which was principally held by the Richmond militia, all day. While at rest, General Lee came riding up, and inquired what troops we were, and upon being told a part of Pickett's division, consisting of the First, Eleventh and Nineteenth Virginia regiments, he said, "All right, I know these men, and they will do their duty."

Late on the 18th we relieved Wright's brigade at Fussell's Mills, where part of us worked on the breastworks and the rest stood guard all night, awaiting an attack in a driving rain. Early the next morning we saw the enemy, posted right in our front on the other side of the millpond, and opened a correspondence with him; that is, we told them not to fire, as they had Pickett's division in their front, to which they cheerfully agreed. One of them was heard to call: " Don't you want to swap the New York *Herald* for the Richmond *Examiner?*" To which Pat Woods, from our side, replied: "And have the *Herald* taken back to New York and let him print the truth in it and we will swap with you;" which was greeted with laughter, in which the Yanks heartily joined. Pretty soon we mingled together, exchanging papers, tobacco and coffee, and not a shot

4

was fired on that part of the line, to the great astonishment of the militia, which were halted in reserve.   On the following morning we found the enemy gone from our front, and we commenced our return march to our camp near Port Walthall, which we reached late on the 20th.

September 14th, moved into a new line of works in our rear; strengthened works and built winter quarters.

On the 18th of October, one of the Seventh regiment men was shot in rear of our company's quarters for deserting.   After the volley was fired, it was found all of the six balls had gone through the centre of his breast and entered the stake to which he was tied, cutting it half in two.

November 28th.   On this morning we discovered that the enemy's pickets consisted of negro troops.   We had, prior to this event, been on the most friendly terms with the enemy's skirmishers.   Trading for coffee and exchanging papers were daily occurrences, but this morning, seeing the black faces in our front, not over three hundred yards off, put a stop to peace and harmony.   About a dozen of us went for them.   Taking our rifles, and without firing a shot, we started for the black line with a yell, and when they saw us coming there was a stampede along the whole line.   Dropping their guns, blankets, canteens and almost everything that was not on their backs, they did not stop running until they reached the main line.   We gathered up everything that was useful and returned without a scratch to our line.

January 8th, 1865, moved to the extreme left of the line near the Howlett House.   On the 22d our gun-boats came down to the Howlett House battery, after passing the enemy's forts, and started towards City Point.   In the attempt to pass the obstructions in our front all except one, the Fredericksburg, ran aground. She succeeded in doing considerable damage to the enemy's vessels.   During that night a heavy demonstration was made by our troops, and the next day the enemy's monitors arrived and opened on our ironclads, which were aground in the river. A small wooden gun-boat, the Drewry, was blown up by them. The firing was quite lively, the forts also, on both sides, taking a hand in it.   About the middle of the day our boats succeeded, without material loss, in retiring to the rear of Fort Howlett, and and at night they returned towards Richmond.

February 20th, the regiment met and passed the following res·
olutions, which shows the spirit of the men, who were ready to
"do and die for their country's sake."   Lieutenant-Colonel Langley acted as chairman, and Lieutenant Jones as secretary :

At a meeting of the officers and men of the First Virginia infantry,
Terry's brigade, Pickett's division, held at their camp near the Howlett
House on the 15th of February, 1865, for the purpose of expressing their
sentiments and determination to devote all of their energy to the prose-
cution of the war, the following resolutions were adopted :

Resolved, That to the humiliating propositions for peace made by
President Lincoln to our companions, we enter our indignant protest ;
that while we would be rejoiced to stop the effusion of blood and the
desolation of our country, we will assent to no terms short of indepen-
dence and separate nationality.

Resolved, That inasmuch as we have tendered the olive branch to our
foes, which they have trampled in the dust, no alternative is left us but
to defend our homes, our property and lives, as long as the foot of a
vandal pollutes the soil of the South.

Resolved, That while recognizing our dependence on Almighty God,
who defends the cause of the just, we again dedicate ourselves to the
cause.   Again we unfurl a banner which we have borne from Bull Run
to Bermuda Hundreds, and again we swear to "die freemen rather than
slaves."

Resolved, That we hail with pleasure the appointment of R. E. Lee
General-in-Chief; that we have an abiding confidence in his judgment,
patriotism and valor, and wherever he orders we will go with joyful
acclamation.

Resolved, That the people at home be exhorted to sustain the army,
to drive back the skulker, to aid in feeding and clothing the soldiers, to
send the best men into councils of the nation, that energy and ability
may be infused into the different departments, State and Confederate.

Resolved, That though disaster and gloom now hovers over us, we
believe all things will be so ordered in the coming campaign, that our
wrongs will be avenged, our rights secured, and those who now claim
us as slaves will own us as victors.

Resolved, That we would hail with acclamation the enrolment into
our armies of Negro troops; we therefore recommend to our repre-
sentatives in Congress assembled, to use their endeavors for the imme-
diate accomplishment of that end.

February 24th, moved back to the right of the line near Swift
Creek.   About eighty recruits were added to the regiment, who,

together with the detailed men returned to their respective companies by the orders of General Lee, filled some of the gaps in
our ranks.   The detailed men, as a general thing, did not relish
this change much.

J. R. Steger, a member of Company D, who met with this fate,
expressed his feelings in the following lines, which he called

"THE BOMB-PROOF'S LAMENT."

With all my heart, I hate to part,
  For I'm not happy to be free;
And it will surely break my heart
  To send me back to Company D.

We had a snug detail together;
  But Uncle Bob has clipped our wings,
And spring will be but gloomy weather
  If doomed to fight old Grant in spring.

Farewell! and when some sickly fellow
  Shall claim this bomb-proof I resign,
And three miles in the rear discover
  What ease and safety once were mine,

I think I should be sweetly blest
  If you for me then would apply;
And tell the General and the rest
  He suits not half so well as I.

About twenty-eight of the recruits, or conscripts, were from
Wythe county.   They formed a company by themselves, as
Company K, under Lieutenant W. M. Lawson, who had lost his
arm while gallantly carrying the colors at Gettysburg.

Among the conscripts was a Russian named Lesafki, who was
remarkable for his great appetite.   He could never get enough
to eat, though he would eat almost anything, ever watching around
wherever there was anything to be had, especially at General
Terry's quarters, where he became a familiar object when cooking
time arrived.   It was usual for several of the men in each company to form a mess, and in drawing rations one of the mess would
draw the rations for all.   Now, poor Lesafki lived by and for
himself alone, and in drawing rations he would see the men come
up and draw five, six, or seven rations each, and he would only
get one.   Not understanding that they drew the rations for the

whole mess, made him think that he was unjustly treated, and he used to complain bitterly, saying (naming the men): A. gets five breads, B., six breads, C., five breads, and naming himself last, Lesafki, *one*. A., five meats, B., six meats, C., five meats, Lesafki, *bone*. But we had more reasonable grounds for complaint against him. Whenever he was on picket duty he would blaze away at every man who would attempt to pass his post, which caused the men to be somewhat shy of him, until some one had the happy idea of silencing his gun by driving a tack in the nipple and breaking it off. At a subsequent skirmish Lesafki was seen to take aim and pull trigger. Pop, pop went the caps, but the gun was no go; it only served as amusement for the boys who stood watching the fun.

With the exception of a few skirmishes in which we participated (two of these occurred during the night, Sergeant J. Q. Figg and myself receiving slight wounds), we had a quiet time on the skirmish line. Drilling, guard and picket duty, and working on the fortifications, were our principal occupation.

On these cold mornings could be heard the voice of our Sergeant-Major, A. J. Simpson, "Turn out here, men, for shivering and frizzing," which was meant for the fatigue detail to work on the *chevaux de frise* in front of the works. About this time the men had learned the value of being protected by the shelter of earthworks, and they could and did do a lot of that work. While around Petersburg and in full view of our camp, the shells were chasing each other through the air, making a beautiful but sometimes dangerous display for the participants. At night the sight was a brilliant exhibition of fire-works.

March 5th. Our (Pickett's) division was relieved by Mahone's division, and put into the field for active duty. The commencement of our move was the starting point of new troubles. After halting near the Petersburg turnpike, within two miles of Chester Station, a cold rain came down and continued for two days.

On the 8th General Pickett held a grand review of his division. The next day we marched to Manchester, and the following day, the 10th, we passed through Richmond and halted in the outer line of works near the Brook road. The next morning moved along the line of works to the Nine-Mile road, and the following day returned to the position near the Brook road.

On the 14th we started about 12 o'clock, and marched within four miles of Ashland, where we halted in line of battle. General Longstreet was in command of the force of which our division was the main part. On the next day the Fifteenth Virginia regiment had a sharp skirmish with Sheridan's cavalry at Ashland. At night we were changing our position, moving about towards the right, and halting every once in awhile, awaiting an attack. The next day we reached the Pamunkey river, and built a bridge, but our pursuit after the enemy's cavalry was useless, as they had disappeared for other parts, and we returned to the lines near the Nine-Mile road.

On the 23d there was another grand review of Pickett's division by General Longstreet.

On the 25th we marched to Richmond, and took the train on the Petersburg road for Dunlop's Station, near which place we camped until the evening of the 29th, when we were ordered to the right flank of Lee's army. Marched to the Appomattox river, which we crossed on the pontoon bridge five miles above Petersburg. Here the three brigades, Stewart's, Corse's and ours (Terry's) took the cars for Sutherland Station, on the Southside railroad, but ours and the Seventh regiment, as was our usual luck, had to walk most of the way that night, and halted near Sutherland's Tavern, on the Cox road, in a drizzling rain. Before daybreak the next morning we were again on the march, and crossing Hatcher's Run, we marched to the extreme right of the lines near Five Forks, where our regiment and the Seventh were thrown out to drive off the enemy's cavalry, who were occupying this position. This we did in a handsome style. At night we were placed on picket duty at this point. On the morning of the 31st we moved on towards the right, in direction of Dinwiddie Courthouse. Found the enemy in heavy force at the crossing of Chamberlayne's Creek, engaged with Fitz. Lee's cavalry. Our brigade, the Third Virginia regiment, in front, effected a crossing somewhat higher up, not, however, without heavy loss to that regiment, the men having to wade the deep creek, on the other side of which the enemy was posted behind works. We followed in pursuit of the enemy, who made several stands, and succeeded in driving him within a mile of Dinwiddie Courthouse, where we came to a halt at night. Our loss was slight. During the day Sergeant J. P. Perrin, of our company, was shot through the head, and died a few weeks afterwards from the effects of his wounds, and Private J. R. Atkinson, of Company G, was wounded.

General Pickett learning that a heavy infantry force was coming to the support of Sheridan's cavalry, which we had been fighting, we were ordered to return. Started about 2 o'clock on the following morning. April 1st, reached Five Forks, where we were placed in line of battle; throwing up some breastworks, just getting ready to fix up something to eat, when we were attacked by the enemy's cavalry in front. The first notice of the enemy's appearance was given by some of our skirmishers running in, who reported the enemy had gobbled up nearly the whole of Company "C," which company was on the skirmish line at the time. Lieutenant R. McC. Jones, who had charge of them, had just returned with a request that the line be reformed, it having been placed in an exposed position, and thereby escaped capture. After finishing our skirmish line the cavalry charged our main line; but here they met with a bloody repulse. Crenshaw's battery, Pegram's battalion, which was posted just at the crossing of the roads, did effective work. Thus the enemy's cavalry was forced to keep a respectful distance.

Meanwhile, Warren's corps of infantry had succeeded in breaking our lines between our position and Petersburg, and gotten in our rear and on our left flank. Our brigade was then withdrawn from the line and made to face the enemy's infantry. Charging them with a yell, which could be heard for miles, we succeeded in driving them some distance, but our ranks were too thin to stand the heavy masses of the enemy's lines, and we were obliged to retire. Our loss was mostly in prisoners; about eighty-five men were captured, one man was killed (J. Wade, of Company H), and a few wounded from the regiment.

PRISONERS.

Field and Staff.—Assistant Surgeon Dr. Sargent.

Company B.—Sergeant J. L. Littlepage; Corporal W. J. Carter.

Company C.—Corporal R. C. Price (wounded); Privates W. H. Brock, J. Bell, James Corcoran, Thomas Collins, H. W. Collins, W. G. Collins; Corporal L. Carrol; Privates Willis Clarke,

W. H. Crenshaw, M. H. Cary, J. D. Clarke, James Edwards, J. M. Gravely, J. H. Goulden, W. P. Ingram, Ab. Jones, J. W. Johnson, Otto Lesafki, P. McCauley, James·McCrossen, B. J McCary, E. R. Maiden, W. D. Miles, Thomas Murphy, M. Nolan, B. R. Nobles, F. R. Noel, G. W. Pollard, A. E. Powell, J. E. Scammel, G. R. Self, T. A. Thorp, A. Truman, James Thomas, J. W. Tillman, N. J. Williams, E. L. White, H. L. Williams.

Company D.—Sergeants J. H. Kepler, C. T. Loehr; Privates W. J. Armstrong, J. N. Andrews, H. C. Bowe, J. G. Braton, J. Draper, J. T. Farmer, D. R. Foushee, P. P. Fuqua, B. K. Garratt, J. Harris, W. P. Mahone, C. L. Nelson, A. Moss, C. M. Sublett, C. Wheeley, S. L. Wingfield.

Company G.—Sergeants Geo. W. Ball, Wm. H. Dean, Thos. W. Hay; Privates Ed. C. Gary (wounded), W. A. Wood.

Company H.—Lieutenant P. C. Cabell; Sergeant Thomas S. Riddick; Privates John Lawson (wounded), N. Bernstein, W. H. Duerson, G. A. Nolting, J. J. Sinnott.

Company I.—Sergeant John T. Crew, W. T. White (wounded); Privates J. L. Ashworth, C. H. Chappell, Harvey Hodges, J. C. Head.

This list is not complete, but contains only such names as the writer has been able to obtain by information.

The majority of the prisoners were sent to Point Lookout, I among this lot, where they arrived on the 5th after a wearisome march of over sixty miles to City Point, and thence by boat. What we here suffered cannot be described. When we landed we were stripped of our overcoats, blankets, oil-cloths, and most of our baggage, which was kicked into the water by the Federal Sergeants who searched us, for the reason that it was United States property, which was true in most cases, for we were armed and clothed by the Federal government, by the battles we had won. After being deprived of nearly all we had to keep us warm, we were put into the bull-pen, as it was called. There were over 23,000 prisoners at Point Lookout at that time, and this number was still further swelled from the prisoners captured on Lee's retreat. The water, the principal substance for a prisoner, was all brackish, owing to the land being only a few feet above the level of the bay, and the food was wholly insufficient. There was little or no medicine for the sick.   Over 6,800 men died at this prison.*   It was not till the middle of June that the United States government saw fit to commence to release us.   A more miserable looking set of men could hardly be produced on an exhibition.   Some of the men were sent to Newport News, and others to Hart Island and other prisons; the officers were forwarded to Johnson's Island.

As to the rest of our regiment, they who were forced to fall back at Five Forks, where they succeeded, after rallying on Corse's brigade, which occupied the right of our line, in maintaining their position, and during the night they were further reinforced by Hunton's brigade, which came from Petersburg.

Early on the morning of the 2d of April, the command marched about twelve miles, and halted at Exeter Mills, on the Appomattox river, thence the division, about 2,200 strong, moved to Deep Creek, which was reached that night, and after a short halt continued the retreat, without rations.   With the exception of about sixty pounds of meal, which our Commissary-Sergeant managed to get hold of, which being distributed gave every man in the regiment about half a pound of bread, there was nothing to be had.   Then came the report of the destruction of Richmond; still the men struggled along, hoping against hope, going they knew not—and most of them cared not—where.

On the night of the 5th the command reached Sailors' Creek and formed in line of battle, throwing up temporary breastworks. The next morning Sheridan's cavalry made several attacks.   The fighting continued until evening, when the enemy's infantry made its appearance in front, while the cavalry swept around our flanks, and thus our little command was entirely surrounded, and Lieutenant-Colonel F. H. Langley surrendered the regiment. Just before the surrender Corporal N. T. Earnest, of Company B, was killed; also Captain Harris, of General Terry's staff.   A few others were wounded.   Below is a partial list of those captured in the regiment:

---

*Among these were W. H. Deane, of Company "G," whose songs had brought life into the men when nearly exhausted on many a weary march. A. Moss (our company cook), and J. Harris, both of Company D, and Private J. W. Gravitt, Company B, also found their untimely end here. At Newport News, Private T. R. Hoffman died.

Field and Staff—Lieutenant-Colonel F. H. Langley; Major G. F. Norton.

Company B.—Captain T. H. Davis; Lieutenant L. S. Robins; Sergeants B. M. Crow, John Q. Figg; Corporal M. P. Buchanan; Privates J. W. Cauthorn, G. R. Heath, Charles Mitchell, J. W. Gravitt, J. A. Green.

Company C.—Sergeant Pat. Woods.

Company D.—Captain E. P. Reeve; Sergeant G. E. Craig; Privates Meyer Angle, Thomas W. Traylor, R. H. Redman, C. L. Pettit, W. R. Wilkins, W. A. Westmoreland.

Company G.—Captain Eldridge Morris; Lieutenant W. T. Woody; Corporal John Allen; Privates E. C. Atkins, Peter Blunt, J. Ryland Epps, C. W. Gentry, A. Jeff. Vaughan.

Company H.—Sergeant R. H. Norvell; Privates J. Belcher, Ro. E. Dignum, Thomas Mouring, William Belcher.

Company I.—Corporal E. G. Loving; Privates T. R. Hoffman, F. R. Pugh, Robert J. Smith, W. P. Smith.

*Company K.**—Lieutenant W. M. Lawson.

A few who were not in line at the time the regiment was captured, and those that were with the wagons ahead, escaped, straggling along until they reached Appomattox Courthouse, behind whose hills the Confederate stars went down to rise no more.

I give below a list of the men who surrendered at Appomattox Courthouse with General Lee. The list was furnished by the War Department at Washington:

Andrew J. Simpson, Sergeant-Major in command; William Harper Deane, Quartermaster-Sergeant; Elias P. Hudgins, Ordnance-Sergeant; James Stagg, John F. Snyder, George C. Hancock, George W. Earnest, John N. Johnson, privates, Company B; Thomas A. Howard, John F. Wheeley, Lamuel R. Wingfield, James P. Mahane, privates, Company D; Private John K. Wilkinson, Company G; Private Robert E. Womack, Company H; Martin Oeters, James A. Jordan, H. S. Carter, privates, Company I. In all, seventeen men.

---

*This company was formed from recruits sent us from Wythe county. I have not been able to get a list of the men.

These were the last of the "Old First," in the war between the States.

I conclude my sketch with an extract from General James L. Kemper's farewell address to his old brigade of May 2d, 1864:

"It is the most painful duty of my life to sever the relations which for three years have harmoniously united us; which have carried us together through memorable and fiery trials, and have bound you to my heart with ties stronger than 'hooks of steel.' No portion of our armies will present to the world more splendid annals of valor than the *First, Third, Seventh, Eleventh,* and *Twenty-fourth,* regiments of Virginia infantry. Let us ever remember, also, as honored comrades, though now separated from us, the noble *Seventeenth* Virginia, identified with us by two years of common toils and achievements. It were enough of honor to have shared the fortunes of any of these regiments. Any soldier might well be proud to possess the command of them all. Stouter heroes have not trod the field of battle. In your torn flags, your scarred persons, your rolls of gallant dead, you bear memorials of a long succession of glorious conflicts; from the smoke and fire of not one of them have you emerged without honor."

LIST OF MEMBERS,

1861-1865.

Ahern, Cornelius,	First year,	Co. C.
Ainsko, Joseph,	1861-63,	I.
Ainsko, John,	1861-63,	I.
Ainsko, Joseph,	1861-62, killed,	I.
Albertson, A. E.,	During the war,	G.
Alexander, Lawrence,	First year,	E.
Allan, William G., Captain and Q. M.,	First year,	F. & S.
Allen, George W., Jr.,	1861, discharged,	G.
Allen, James,	1861, discharged,	I.
Allen, John E.,	1861, killed,	B.
Allen, John,	During the war,	G.
Allen, Ro. B.,	1861, discharged,	G.
Alluisi, Julian,	First year,	K.
Alport, John F.,	During the war,	G.
Anderson, H. T.,	1861, discharged,	I.
Anderson, W. N.,	During the war,	H.
Andrew, J. N.,	1863, to the end,	D.
Angle, J. B.,	During the war,	D.
Angle, Meyer,	1864, to the end,	D.
Archer, James W., Lieutenant,	1861, resigned,	B.
Armstrong, J. H.,	1861, discharged,	G.
Armstrong, R. E., Sergeant,	During the war,	H.
Armstrong, William J.,	During the war,	D.
Armstrong, William R.,	1861, discharged,	G.
Arzberger, Charles,	First year,	K.
Asher, Louis,	1861, discharged,	H.
Ashby, B. F.,	During the war,	G.
Ashby, H. C.,	1861, detached,	G.
Ashby, Robert,	1861, discharged,	G.
Ashby, R. A.,	1863, to the end,	I.
Ashworth, John,	1863, to the end,	I.
Atkins, E. C.,	During the war,	G.
Atkinson, John,	1861,	G.
Atkinson, J. Rosser,	During the war,	G.
Ayres, J. T.,	1861-1864, detached,	I.
Alrich, W. A., Chaplain,	1862,	F. & S.
Ball, George W., Sergeant,	During the war,	G.

Ball, William,	1861, detached,	Co. H.
Ballentine, J. W.,	1861, detached,	H.
Balliew, T. W.	1861–63, discharged,	I.
Balliew, William T.,	1864, to the end,	I.
Ballow, Henry C., Lieutenant,	During the war,	I.
Banks, Sol.,	1862–63, in prison,	H.
Barker, John R.,	First year,	E.
Barker, William N.,	First year,	E.
Barnes, M. A.,	1861, killed,	H.
Barry, James,	First year,	E.
Bass, W. U.,	1861, discharged,	D.
Bates, Joseph W.,	During the war,	D.
Bauman, C., Lieutenant,	First year,	K.
Beale, C. D., Sergeant,	1861–62, killed,	B.
Beale, John H.,	1861, discharged,	B.
Beazley, R.,	1862,	D.
Belcher, I.,	1863, to the end,	H.
Belcher, William,	1863, to the end,	H.
Belesario, E.,	1862,	D.
Bell, Jeremiah,	1863, to the end,	C.
Bell, ——,	1865, to the end,	G.
Bergmeier, B.,	First year,	K.
Bernaugh, G. D.,	First year,	E.
Betts, R. S., Corporal,	1861, detached,	H.
Berry, Alexander,	First year,	Drummer.
Bitzel, Adam,	1861, discharged,	K.
Black, Robert,	1863,	G.
Bladen, ——,	First year,	Drummer.
Blair, Ad., Lieutenant,	1861–64, disabled,	D.
Blankenship, R.,	1864, to the end,	D.
Blanton, L. M., Lieutenant,	During the war,	D. & C.
Blenkner, G.,	First year,	K.
Blenkner, Julius,	First year,	K.
Blunt, Peter,	1865, to the end,	G.
Bodeker, G. H.,	1862,	B.
Boggs, F. J., Captain,	1861, resigned,	H.
Bohannan, William A.,	1861–62, died,	B.
Boland, John,	1861, detached,	C.
Boler, G. W.,	1862, to the end,	I.
Bolton, W.,	First year,	Drummer.
Boltz, August,	1861, detached,	B.
Boltz, Henry,	1861, detached,	B.
Bonn, George E.,	First year,	H.
Bonn, Henry R.,	First year,	H.
Bonn, Joseph, Corporal,	First year,	H.
Booker, ——,	1864, died,	H.

Bornickel, John W.,	First year,	Co. K.
Bottoms, S. D.,	First year,	D.
Botzen, L.,	First year,	K.
Boucher, H.,	1861, detached,	D.
Boucher, John,	First year,	Band.
Bowe, H. C.,	1864, to the end,	D.
Bowe, Nat. W.,	During the war,	D.
Boyden, James J.,	First year,	B.
Boyle, D. Jackson,	First year,	E.
Bradford, H.,	First year,	E.
Brannon, Frank,	First year,	Drummer.
Braton, J. G.,	1863, to the last,	D.
Braw, John,	1861-62, died,	K.
Bray, James L., Sergeant,	1861, discharged,	H.
Breeden, W. F.,	1861, discharged,	D.
Brissacher, C.,	First year,	K.
Bresnahan, M.,	1863, killed,	H.
Bresnahan, M.,	1861,	C.
Bridgeford, D. B., Commissary,	1861,	F & S.
Brighthaupt, G.,	First year,	E.
Brimmer, H.,	1861,	G.
Brock, W. H.,	1864, to the end,	C.
Brooks, Fayette,	1861, discharged,	B.
Brooks, H.,	1861-62, killed,	I.
Brotherton, D. H.,	First year,	H.
Brown, J. T.,	1861, discharged,	H.
Browne, T. S.,	First year,	E.
Brown, Theo.,	1861, detached,	B.
Brown, Valentine, Jr.,	First year, transferred,	D.
Brunner, R.,	1861,	K.
Bryant, J. E.,	1861, discharged,	G.
Buchannan, M. P., Corporal,	During the war,	B.
Buchenan, Conrad,	First year,	K.
Buchenan, Henry,	First year,	K.
Buckley, James,	First year,	Band.
Buckley, William,	During the war,	C.
Birch, J. E.,	First year,	E.
Burch, George,	First year,	Drummer.
Burgess, A. A.,	1862, killed,	I.
Burke, William J.,	First year,	C.
Burkhard, Henry, Corporal,	First year,	K.
Burnett, J. W.,	1861,	B.
Burns, T. C., Sergeant,	1861, discharged,	C.
Bernstein, N.,	1864, to the end,	H.
Burton, Ro. C.,	1861, discharged,	D.

Burton, H. W., Corporal,	1861, transferred,	Co. D.
Burton, Marion,	1864, to the end,	H.
Butler, R. L.,	1861, discharged,	G
Butler, ——, Assistant-Surgeon,	First year,	F. & S.
Butt, George,	First year,	E.
Byrne, Ed.,	First year,	C.
Byron, John,	1863, to the last,	B.
Cabell, P. C., Lieutenant,	During the war,	H.
Cabell, William M.,	1865,	H.
Caho, William A., Lieutenant,	1861–63, killed,	I.
Callahan, John E.,	First year,	E.
Camp, James W.,	During the war,	H.
Carr, James V.,	First year,	C.
Carroll, Lawrence, Corporal,	During the war,	C.
Carter, C. C.,	1861–62, killed,	B.
Carter, H. S.,	1864, to the end,	I.
Carter, R. L.,	1864, died,	I.
Carter, William J., Corporal,	During the war,	B.
Carey, M. H.,	1863, to the end,	C.
Carver, J. F.,	First year,	E.
Casey, Pat.,	First year,	C.
Castello, Tim., Corporal,	1861, discharged,	C.
Cauthorn, J. W.,	1862, to the end,	B.
Chaddick, J. J.,	1861–62, disabled,	H.
Chaddick, Richard, Corporal,	1861–63, killed,	H.
Chamberlayne, E. H. Jr., Sergeant,	1861, discharged,	D.
Chaney, ——,	1864,	G.
Chappell, A. A.,	1861–64, killed,	I.
Chappell, C. H.,	1863, to the end,	I.
Chappell, J. F.,	1861–63, died,	I.
Chappell, William T.,	1861,	I.
Charles, John H., Corporal,	1861, discharged,	B.
Childress, Thad.,	1861, discharged,	G.
Childrey, John H.,	First year,	B.
Chilton, William B.,	First year,	E.
Chockley, W. E.,	First year,	D.
Claggett, Maurice,	First year,	H.
Clarke, H. C.,	1861, discharged,	H.
Clarke, J. D.,	1864, to the end,	C.
Clarke, John T., Sergeant,	First year,	E.
Clarke, John T.,	1861,	B.
Clarke, S.,	1863,	I.
Clarke, Willis,	1864, to the end,	C.
Clash, C. V.,	1861, discharged,	H.
Clayton, Allen O.,	During the war,	H.
Clayton, R. J.,	1861, died,	H.

Cleary, James K.,	First year,	Co. E.
Clifford, Thomas C.,	First year,	C.
Cobb, James H., Lieutenant,	First year, resigned,	B.
Cole, W. H.,	First year,	E.
Collier, E. J., Jr.,	1861, discharged,	D.
Collins, Cor.,	1861, discharged,	I.
Collins, Thomas,	During the war,	C.
Collins, H. W.,	1864, to the end,	C.
Collins, M.,	1863,	I.
Collins, Thomas,	First year,	E.
Collins, W. G.,	1863, to the end,	C.
Connor, James,	1861, discharged,	C.
Connor, James,	First year,	E.
Consadine, Michael,	1861–64, killed,	C.
Cook, J. C.,	1864, to the end,	D.
Cook, Stephen J.,	First year,	E.
Cook, William F.,	1861, discharged,	G.
Copenhofer, G. A.,	1861,	H.
Corcoran, James,	During the war,	C.
Cordle, R. E.,	1863, died,	I.
Cornick, George C.,	1861, discharged,	I.
Corr, G. W.,	1864, to the end,	D.
Costican, J. M.,	1861,	D.
Cox, ——,	1861,	H.
Craddock, R. B.,	1861, detached,	G.
Craig, George E., Sergeant,	During the war,	D.
Creamer, Patrick,	First year,	C.
Cree, William E.,	First year,	K.
Creedins, C. W.,	First year,	K.
Crenshaw, T. E.,	First year, transferred,	D.
Crenshaw, W. H.,	1863, to the end,	C.
Crew, John T., Sergeant,	During the war,	I.
Cromwell, S. A.,	First year,	E.
Crow, B. M., Sergeant,	During the war,	B.
Crowe, D. N.,	1861, discharged,	H.
Crowe, George W.,	1861, detached,	D.
Crump, Robert A., Corporal,	1861, discharged,	G.
Crigger, W. H.,	1862–64, killed,	B.
Cullen, J. S. D., Surgeon,	1861, transferred,	F. & S.
Cullingsworth, William H.,	First year,	G.
Cumby, Major,	1864,	D.
Cummings, Pat.,	1861, discharged,	C.
Cunningham, F. D., Ass't Surgeon,	1861, transferred,	F. & S.
Dabney, J. E.,	1861–63,	I.
Dabney, V.,	1861, transferred,	D.
Daley, Mich.,	1861,	C.

Daniel, John H.,	During the war,	Co. H.
Daniels, Joseph,	1862, to the end,	B.
Dansey, John A., Corporal,	First year,	G.
Davidge, J. B.,	First year,	E.
Davidson, E. F.,	1862, to the end,	H.
Davis, B. T.,	1861, discharged,	B.
Davis, E. M.,	1863, to the end,	C.
Davis, John R.,	First year,	H.
Davis, Richard T.,	1861, discharged,	B.
Davis, T. Herbert, Captain,	During the war,	B.
Davis, T. S.,	First year,	D.
Davis, Thomas K.,	First year,	E.
Davis, W. A.,	1861, transferred,	H.
Dawson, James,	1864,	H.
Dawson, R. Joseph,	First year,	E.
Dean, William H., Sergeant,	During the war,	G.
Dean, Wm. Harper, Sergeant,	During the war,	B.
DeBar, D.,	First year,	K.
Deekman, George F., Sergeant,	First year,	K.
Degenhart, C. P.,	1861, disabled,	K.
Delamonte, L.,	1862,	B.
Delaway, W. H.,	First year,	H.
Denegri, J. B.,	First year, detached,	D.
Dennis, S. C.,	1862, to the end,	H.
Dennis, James,	1863, to the end,	C.
Devoux, J. F.,	1861-62, prisoner,	I.
Diacont, Adam,	First year,	K.
Diacont, Philip,	First year,	K.
Diacont, Wolfgang,	1861, killed,	K.
Dick, John T.,	First year,	K.
Dignum, R. E.,	During the war,	H.
Dilger, Joseph,	First year,	K.
Doll, John,	1861,	B.
Donahoe, John, Lieutenant,	1861-62, killed,	C.
Donahoe, Charles R.,	First year,	E.
Dooley, James H.,	1862, disabled,	C.
Dooley, John, Major,	First year,	C. and F. & S.
Dooley, John E., Captain,	1862, to the end,	D. & C.
Doran, Phillip, Sergeant,	1861, discharged,	C.
Dorin, Michael B., Sergeant,	1861, detached,	C.
Dove, Robert,	First year,	E.
Doyle, Benjamin,	1863-64,	Drummer.
Draper, John,	1863, to the end,	D.
Driscoll, James W.,	1861, killed,	C.
Dubel, Henry,	1861, disabled,	K.
Duerson, W. H.,	1862, to the end,	H.

Duffey, Patrick, Corporal,	First year,	Co. C.
Duke, H. T.,	1863, to the end,	I.
Duncan, William M.,	1861, discharged,	B.
Dunn, James,	1861,	C.
Dunn, R. N., Corporal,	During the war,	H.
Durham, Thomas, Sergeant,	1861-63, disabled,	G.
Dwyer, T. R.,	First year,	E.
Earle, John,	First year,	E.
Earnest, N. T., Corporal,	1861-65, killed,	B.
Earnest, George W.,	1864, to the end,	B.
Edwards, James,	1864, to the end,	C.
Edwards, David S.,	1861-63, killed,	D.
Edwards, George T.,	First year,	E.
Eggleston, W. B.,	1861, detached,	H.
Ellett, L. O., Corporal,	1861-63, killed,	I.
Ellig, John,	First year,	Band.
Elsasser, H. T., Sergeant,	First year,	K.
Emmerson, R.,	First year,	Band.
Emmenhauser, John,	1861, discharged,	K.
Emory, Marion,	1861, discharged,	B.
England, George,	1865, to the end,	G.
English, William, Captain,	First year,	C.
Ennis, P. J., Sergeant,	First year,	E.
Enright, Michael,	First year,	C.
Epps, J. R.,	During the war,	G.
Esby, James,	First year,	E.
Estres, W. C.,	First year,	H.
Eubank, ——,	1862,	H.
Eubank, George,	First year,	Drummer.
Euker, Charles, Corporal,	1861, transferred,	B.
Evans, D.,	First year,	I.
Eubank, G. W.,	1861-63,	I.
Fagan, James,	1861, discharged,	C.
Fahrenbruch, Aug.,	First year,	K.
Farmer, J. T.,	1862, to the end,	D.
Farrar, James,	During the war,	G.
Farson, S.,	1861, prisoner,	H.
Fergusson, H. C.,	1861-63, disabled,	G.
Fergusson, Robert A.,	During the war,	G.
Fergusson, W. J.,	During the war,	G.
Ferneyhough, E. M., Corporal,	1861-62, killed,	D.
Ferneyhough, E. S.,	1861, discharged,	D.
Freslow, William E., Sergeant,	1861, discharged,	B.
Figg, John Q., Sergeant,	During the war,	B.
Figner, A., Corporal,	1861-64, killed,	I.
Fink, John,	1861, discharged,	K.

Finn, J. M., Sergeant,	1861–63, prisoner,	Co. D.
Finnerty, John,	First year,	C.
Fitzgerald, Edward,	First year,	C.
Fitzgerald, John E., Corporal,	First year,	E.
Fizer, E.,	1862–63, prisoner,	H.
Flaherty, James F.,	First year,	E.
Fleckenstein, H.,	First year,	K.
Flemming, M.,	First year,	C.
Flowers,	1862–63, killed,	H.
Foley,	1863,	G.
Ford, F.,	1862,	B.
Ford, F. H.,	1861,	H.
Ford, John,	1864, to the end,	I.
Fore, V. L., Lieutenant,	1861, resigned,	I.
Foresighte, A. W.,	1861, disabled,	C.
Foster, D.,	1863,	H.
Foushee, D. R.,	1863, to the end,	D.
Fowlkes, C. C., Sergeant,	1861–62, killed,	G.
Fox, A.,	1864, died,	D.
Fox, Richard,	First year,	Band.
Frankenthal, S.,	First year,	B.
Franklin, F.,	1861–63, killed,	B.
Fawley, John,	1861, died,	C.
Frayser, D.,	First year,	I.
Freeman, J. W..	1862–63, killed,	D.
Firth, J. A.,	1861–62, killed,	D.
Fry, William H., Lieut.-Colonel,	1861, detached,	F. & S.
Fry, W. T., Adjutant,	1861–62, detached,	F. & S.
Fuqua, P. P.,	1863, to the end,	D.
Furbush, ——,	1863, to the end,	G.
Furcron, Henry W., Corporal,	During the war,	D.
Gardiner, ——, Chaplain,	1863,	F. & S.
Gaffney, L.,	First year, discharged,	C.
Gallagher, J. B.,	1861, discharged,	D.
Gannon, A.,	First year,	C.
Garrett, B. K.,	During the war,	D.
Gartland, Frank,	First year,	E.
Gary, Edwin C.,	During the war,	G.
Gary, Hezekiah B.,	During the war,	G.
Gehring, Joseph,	1861, discharged,	K.
Gelnhausen, L.,	1861, discharged,	K.
Gentry, Charles W.,	During the war,	G.
Gentry, James A.,	1861, detached,	H.
Gentry, James W.,	First year,	K.
Gerhardt, C. C.,	1861, discharged,	I.
Gerhardt, F. J.,	1861,	K.

Gersdorf, George,	1861, detached,	Co. K.
Giannini, F. W.,	First year, discharged,	D.
Giblin, James,	First year, discharged,	C.
Gills, J.,	1864, died,	D.
Gilman, Edwin,	1861–62, disabled,	H.
Gilman, J. D.,	1861,	H.
Ginty, Thomas,	1861,	C.
Glass, George,	First year,	K.
Glinn, G. R.,	1861–62, disabled,	I.
Goddin, G. G., Corporal,	1861–62, killed,	B.
Goodwin, W.,	1861, discharged,	I.
Goodall, J. M.,	1862,	I.
Goodson, E. C., Sergeant,	During the war,	I.
Gordon, W. H., Captain,	First year, retired,	G.
Goulden, J. H.,	1863, to the last,	C.
Goetze, E. A.,	1861,	B.
Govan, Archie,	1862-64, killed,	D.
Grady, James,	First year,	E.
Grammer, J. G.,	1861–62, killed,	I.
Gravitt, J. W.,	1862–65, died in prison,	B.
Gray, Henry,	1862–64, detailed,	B.
Gravely, J. M.,	1863, to the last,	C.
Greaner, J. H., Captain,	First year, retired,	H.
Green, James A.,	1862, to the end,	B.
Green, J. F,	1861, discharged,	I.
Green, W. C.,	First year, discharged,	I.
Griffin, E. J.,	1863, killed,	I.
Grigsby, A. S., Surgeon,	1862, to the end,	F. & S.
Grill, George, Jr.,	1861, discharged,	I.
Griswold, J. G., Captain,	First year, retired,	D.
Gronwald, C. E., Quarterm'r-Serg't,	1861, discharged,	K.
Grossman, E.,	First year,	K.
Gunn, T. H., Corporal,	First year,	G.
Gutbier, Fred.,	1861, killed,	K.
Guy, John H., Corporal,	1861, transferred,	B.
Gillespie, Samuel,	1863-64, killed,	C.
Haake, Gerhard, Sergeant,	First year,	K.
Habermehl, G.,	1861, discharged,	K.
Hach, Fred.,	First year,	K.
Hach, John,	First year,	K.
Hackman, B. F.,	1861, discharged,	D.
Haderman, H.,	First year,	K.
Hagemeyer, F. W., Captain,	First year,	K.
Hahn, P.,	1861–62, discharged,	I.
Haley, John,	1861, discharged,	C.
Haley, Pat.,	1861, discharged,	C.

Haley, T. H.,	1861–62, discharged,	Co. D.
Hall, R. L.,	1864,	D.
Hancock, George C.,	1862, to the end,	B.
Holloran, James, Captain,	1861–63, killed,	C.
Hamilton, John,	1861,	C.
Hamilton, Theo.,	1861, detached,	G.
Hammill, H. J.,	First year,	H.
Hammill, R. S.,	First year,	H.
Hansford, C. P., Sergeant,	1861–63, killed,	H.
Hargrove, B.,	1863, to the end,	C.
Harney, Henry, Lieutenant,	1861, transferred.	D.
Harrington, Pat.,	1861, discharged.	C.
Harris, John,	1864–65, died in prison,	D.
Harris, Hez.,	First year, detached,	D.
Harris, Fred.,	First year,	Drummer.
Harris, P. W.,	1861,	B.
Harrison, Randolph, Captain,	1861, resigned,	B.
Harrison, W. W., Lieutenant,	1861, resigned,	B.
Hart, John,	1864, to the end,	G.
Hartman, F. W.,	1862,	B.
Hartman, J. H.,	1861, discharged,	H.
Harvey, Charles,	1864, to the end,	G.
Harvie, W. O., Sergeant-Major,	1861, transferred,	F. & S.
Haskins, A.,	During the war,	G.
Haskins, George,	1861–62, discharged,	G.
Hassett, Pat.,	1861, discharged,	C.
Havenner, Charles,	First year,	E.
Hay, H. P.,	First year,	B.
Hay, Thomas W., Sergeant,	During the war,	G.
Hazlewood, Joseph,	1863, to the end,	B.
Head, J. C.,	During the war,	I.
Heath, George R.,	During the war,	B.
Hebring, Fred., Sergeant,	First year,	K.
Heinemann, H.,	First year,	K.
Helwick, J. L.,	1861, detached,	K.
Hendricks, J. P.,	1864, died,	D.
Henicke, F. A.,	1861–62,	H.
Henning, C. M.,	First year,	E.
Henry, L. H.,	First year,	E.
Herzog, E.,	First year,	K.
Higgins, Daniel,	1861, discharged,	C.
Hinton, Assistant Surgeon,	1861, discharged,	F. & S.
Hirschberg, Joseph,	First year,	Band.
Hitchcock, R. F.,	First year,	B.
Hite, W. C.,	1862–63, killed,	H.
Hoare, James,	1864, to the end,	C.

Holzmann, S.,	1861–62,	Co. I.
Hoch, A.,	First year,	K.
Hodges, Harvey,	1864, to the end,	I.
Hodges, M.,	1864, to the end,	I.
Hodges, V. E.,	During the war,	G.
Hoffman, Charles,	First year, transferred,	G.
Hoffman, John P.,	First year,	K.
Hollingsworth, R. P.,	1864, to the end,	C.
Hogstett, J. McC.,	1863,	I.
Hooker, J. G.,	1861–62,	I.
Hord, B. H.,	1861–62, disabled,	G.
Hord, William F.,	During the war,	G.
Horner, James E.,	1861, detached,	H.
Hatke, Andrew,	First year,	K.
Hough, O. R., Sergeant,	First year,	H.
Howard, Benjamin F., Captain,	During the war,	I.
Howard, Joseph W.,	1861, discharged,	D.
Howard, Thomas A.,	During the war,	D.
Howry, J. W.,	1861–62,	D.
Hudgins, E. P., Sergeant,	During the war,	G.
Hudnut, E. A.,	1861, discharged,	G.
Huffman, T. R.,	1862–65, died in prison,	I.
Hugel, L. M.,	1861–62, discharged,	I.
Hughes, M.,	1861, disabled,	C.
Hundley J. C.,	1863, discharged,	I.
Hutcheson, W.,	1861,	C.
Ish, M. A.,	1861–64, detached,	I.
Ingram, W. P.,	1863, to the end,	C.
Jackson, John D.,	During the war,	G.
Jackson, T. E.,	1861,	H.
Jackson, W. M.,	1861–62, killed,	H.
Jacobs, John, Jr.,	1861–63, discharged,	B.
Jacobs, Joseph,	1861–62, discharged,	H.
James, D.,	1862,	B.
James, Edwin,	First year,	H.
James, J. H.,	1864, disabled,	I.
James, R. W., Sergeant,	1861, discharged,	I.
Jarboe, G. B.,	First year,	E.
Jarvis, D. A.,	During the war,	D.
Jenkins, C. H.,	1861–62, discharged,	I.
Jennings, J. C., Commissary Sergeant,	During the war,	D.
Johnson, B. C.,	First year,	E.
Johnson, J. W.,	1863, to the end,	C.
Johnson, George W.,	1861–63, disabled,	D.
Johnson, James W.,	1863–64, transferred,	Drummer.
Jones, Abram,	1863, to the end,	C.

Jones, E. B.,	1861, discharged,	Co. D
Jones, John N.,	1864, to the end,	B.
Jones, R. McC., Lieutenant,	During the war,	D. & C.
Jones, R. M., Sergeant,	1861–62, disabled,	I.
Jones, T. R.,	1861, detached,	G.
Jones, William,	1861,	B.
Jordan, E.,	1861–62, discharged,	H.
Jordon, Richard D., Corporal,	During the war,	G.
Jordon, Joseph A.,	1864, to the end,	I.
Jordan, ——,	1862, killed,	B.
Joseph, Wilson B.,	1861–64, disabled,	H.
Joy, George,	1863–64, detached,	I.
Joyce, John,	1861, discharged,	C.
Judge John M.,	First year,	E.
Justice, J. P.,	1864, detached,	D.
Kahn, M.,	First year,	I.
Kavenaugh, John,	1861, disabled,	C.
Kayton, H. H.,	1861, killed,	B.
Kean, Charles,	1861, died,	C.
Kearney, M.,	First year,	C.
Keating, Pat.,	1861–62, killed,	C.
Keiningham, J. C.,	1863, to the end,	D.
Keiningham, Wm. H. (Peter), Lieut.,	During the war,	D.
Kehoe, M.,	1861, discharged,	C.
Kelly, J. C.,	During the war,	I.
Kelly, T. R.,	1862–64, prisoner,	I.
Kendrick, W. F.,	1861–64,	G.
Kennedy, J. A. B.,	1861, discharged,	I.
Kennedy, Joseph,	1861,	C.
Kepler, J. H., Sergeant,	During the war,	D.
Kepler, N.,	1861,	B.
Kieley, J. D.,	1861, detached,	C.
Kilby, W. R.,	1861–63, disabled,	H.
Kessler, Nat.,	1861, disabled,	B.
King, David, Lieutenant,	1861, resigned,	C.
King, E. H.,	1861, discharged,	D.
King, W. H.,	1861, detached,	H.
Knauff, G. F.,	1861, discharged,	G.
Koch, George,	1861, detached,	K.
Kuhn, L. P.,	1861, detached,	H.
Lacy, T. A.,	1861, detached,	I.
Lafong, E. O.,	1862–63, detached,	H.
Lamb, George,	1862,	I.
Lambert, G. W.,	1861,	G.
Landers, R.	1861–62, discharged,	C.
Langley, Frank H., Lieut.-Colonel,	During the war,	G. & F. & S.

Larkins, M.,	1861, discharged,	Co. C.
Lawrence, James,	1862, discharged,	H.
Lauterbach, Fred.,	First year,	K.
Lawson, John,	1864, to the end,	H.
Lawson, M. C.,	1864, to the end,	H.
Lawson, William M., Lieutenant,	During the war,	H.
Layard, William S.,	1861, transferred,	G.
Lee, George W.,	1861, discharged,	D.
Lee, James K, Captain,	1861, killed,	B.
Lee, John W.,	1861-62, transferred,	D.
Lee, Richard,	1863,	C.
Lehmkul, Fred.,	1861, discharged,	K.
Leidey, S. M.,	1861, detached,	G.
Lesafki, Otto,	1864, to the end,	C.
Lester, T. P.,	1863, to the end,	I.
Liggon, John L.,	1861, detached,	G.
Lichtenstein, I.,	1861, discharged,	H.
Lindner, Charles,	1861, detached,	K.
Lindsey, J. J.,	1861, discharged,	G.
Linkhauer, H., Lieutenant,	1861,	K.
Lintz, Samuel,	First year,	E.
Lipscombe, John T.,	1861, detached,	D.
Lipscombe, W. H., Sergeant,	During the war,	I.
Littlepage, J. L., Sergeant,	During the war,	B.
Lloyd, J. A.,	First year,	E.
Lloyd, J. G.,	1863, to the end,	I.
Lloyd, Mathew,	1861, prisoner,	H.
Lloyd, Robert,	1861, prisoner,	H.
Loehr, Charles T., Sergeant,	During the war,	D.
Loehr, Fred.,	1862, disabled and detached,	B.
Logan, George,	1861-62, killed,	D.
Lohmann, F. W. E., Lieutenant,	1861, resigned,	K.
Lord, J. R.,	1861,	G.
Loving, E. B., Corporal,	During the war,	I.
Lucas, T. H.,	1864,	D.
Lucke, B.,	First year,	K.
Lukeman, R.,	First year,	E.
Lumpkin, G. A.,	1861, discharged,	G.
Lumpkin, William J., Sergeant,	1861, disabled,	B.
Lutz, Fred.,	1861,	B.
Lyneman, A. H.,	1861-62, detached,	B.
Lytle, W. A.,	1861-62, detached,	B.
McCabe, H. D.,	1861,	H.
McCabe, L.,	1861, detached,	C.
McCauley, P.,	During the war,	C.
McCann, M.,	1861,	C.

McCary, B. J.,	1863, to the end,	Co. C.
McCarthy, Daniel,	First year,	C.
McCarthy, Mike,	1861,	C.
McCrossen, James,	During the war,	C.
McDonald, John, Sergeant,	1861, detached,	C.
McDonald, John, Lieutenant,	First year, resigned,	G.
McDonough, Thomas,	First year,	Drummer.
McGee, Joseph,	1862, to the end,	H.
McGee, Pat.,	1861, detached,	C.
McGrady, William C.,	1861,	C.
McGlochlin, H.,	First year,	E.
McGrail, P.,	1861–62, disabled,	I.
McGuigon, E.,	1864,	I.
McKaigg, W. W., Lieutenant,	First year,	I.
Mackey, John, Jr.,	1861, discharged,	I.
McLaughlan, H.,	1863, killed,	I.
McLaughlin, H.,	First year,	E.
McLear, J. M.,	1863, to the end,	I.
McMahan, John,	First year,	C.
McMahan, Stephen,	First year,	C.
McMillan, ——,	1861,	D.
McMinn, Delaware,	1861–64, killed,	D.
McMullen, James,	1861,	C.
McNamara, F.,	1861, detached,	C.
McNamee, J. F., Sergeant,	First year,	E.
McNamee, Thomas,	First year,	E.
McPherson, H. S.,	First year,	E.
McRichards, S., Sergeant,	1861, discharged,	C.
Mahane, James R.,	1861,	G.
Mahane, M. R.,	1861–62, killed,	G.
Mahane, William P.,	1862, to the end,	D.
Mahoney. J. E.,	1861, discharged,	H.
Mahoney, Martin,	1861, discharged,	C.
Mallory, S. R.,	1861, killed,	G.
Mallory, C. A.,	First year,	E.
Mallory, W. A.,	During the war,	B.
Mann, F. M., Lieutenant,	1861–62, killed,	B.
Maiden, E. R.,	1863, to the end,	C.
Marooney, P.,	First year,	C.
Marran, James E.,	1861, killed,	E.
Martin, E. W., Lieutenant,	1861–64, disabled,	H.
Martin, R. W. S.,	1861–62, discharged,	H.
Martin, Theo. R., Sergeant,	During the war,	H.
Martin, ——, Chaplain,	1863,	F. & S.
Matthews, N. G.,	1862,	I.
Maury, Thos. F., Assistant-Surgeon,	First year, transferred,	F. & S.

Maxwelll, William, Lieutenant,	First year,	Co. E.
Mayo, D. E.,	1861, discharged,	D.
Mead, Charles,	First year,	E.
Meanley, John A.,	1861-62, disabled,	H.
Meenley, George L., Corporal,	During the war,	D.
Melson, C. L.,	1863, to the end,	D.
Melton, James M.,	First year,	Band.
Mercer, Thomas H., Lieutenant,	1862, disabled,	F. & S.
Meredith, R. O.,	1861-64, detached,	I.
Merkel, Tobias,	First year,	K.
Mesco, John,	1861-62, detached,	B.
Meyer, Felix,	First year,	K.
Meyer, L. V.,	1861, discharged,	D.
Meyer, Max.,	1861-62, discharged,	B.
Michols, Ab.,	1861,	H.
Miles, H. H., Lieutenant,	1861, killed,	G.
Miles, Marion,	1861-62, detached,	D.
Miles, Thomas,	During the war,	G.
Miles, W. D.,	1863, to the end,	C.
Miller, A. W.,	First year,	E.
Miller, C. E.,	1861,	C.
Miller, E. R.,	1861, disabled,	D.
Miller, Florence, Captain,	1861, resigned,	K.
Miller, J. P.,	1861, discharged,	H.
Miller, W. F.,	1861-63, killed,	G.
Mills, R. N., Sergeant,	1861, discharged,	B.
Mills, Robert,	1861,	H.
Minor, A. Thomas,	During the war,	I.
Mitchel, James C.,	1861, discharged,	G.
Mitchell, Charles,	During the war,	B.
Mitchell, George W.,	During the war,	D.
Mitchell, James, Captain,	1861-62, transferred,	C.
Mitchell, J. H.,	1864,	D.
Mitchell, Samuel P., Lieutenant,	1861, transferred,	B.
Mitchell, Willie,	1862-63, killed,	D.
Montague, A.,	1861, died,	H.
Moore, P. T., Colonel,	First year, retired,	F. & S.
Moore, William,	1861, discharged,	C.
Moore, William H.,	1862-63,	I.
Morgan, John H.,	1861, disabled,	H.
Morgan, ——,	1862, to the end,	H.
Moriarty, John, Sergeant,	During the war,	C.
Morris, Eldridge, Captain,	During the war,	G.
Morrice, Isidore, Corporal,	1861, killed,	E.
Morris R. F., Captain,	1861, resigned,	I.
Morris, W. A., Sergeant,	1861-62, killed,	D.

Morrisett, R. C., Corporal,	During the war,	Co. I.
Morton, T. S.,	1861–63, disabled,	D.
Mosby, W. B.,	1862–63, disabled,	H.
Moss, Alexander,	1862–65, died in prison,	D.
Moss, Peter,	1862, killed,	B.
Moss, R. J.,	1862, killed,	I.
Mouney, F.,	First year,	E.
Mountcastle, Geo.,	1861, transferred,	G.
Mountcastle, Oliver,	1861, discharged,	B.
Mountjoy, John,	1861, discharged,	B.
Mouring, Thomas,	During the war,	H.
Mullen, A. P.,	First year,	E.
Mullen, William H.,	First year,	B.
Munford, William, Major,	1861, transferred,	F. & S.
Murphy, Michael,	1861, discharged,	C.
Murphy, John,	1863,	C.
Murphy, Thomas,	During the war,	C.
Murrell, G. W.,	1863–64,	I.
Nagle, Thomas,	1861, detached,	C.
Nagelsmann, Joseph,	1861, detached,	K.
Neal, S. S.,	1863, prisoner,	I.
Neale, George C.,	First year,	E.
New, C. R.,	1861–62, killed,	H.
Newby, ——,	1863,	G.
Noel, F. R.,	1863, to the end,	C.
Noble, N.,	1861, discharged,	G.
Nobles, B. R.,	1863, to the end,	C.
Nolan, Thomas,	1862,	G.
Nolan, Michael,	1863, to the end,	C.
Nolting, G. A.,	During the war,	H.
Noonan, Pat.,	First year,	C.
Norton, George F., Major,	During the war,	D. & F. & S.
Norvell, R. H., Sergeant,	During the war,	H.
Notte, David,	First year,	K.
Notte, Henry,	First year,	K.
Notte, Herman,	First year,	K.
Nuckols, ——,	1862–63, killed,	H.
O'Brien, N.,	First year,	E.
O'Brien, Pat.,	1862,	B.
O'Brien, Pat.,	1861,	C.
Ocker, Joseph,	1861, detached,	K.
Offatt, John R.,	First year,	E.
Offatt, George W., Lieutenant,	First year,	E.
Offatt, Z. A.,	First year,	E.
Ogden, L. W., Sergeant,	During the war,	B.
O'Hare, ——,	1862,	D.

O'Keeffe, James H.,	First year,	Drummer.
O'Keefe, John,	1861, discharged,	C.
O'Keefe, Arthur,	1861, discharged,	C.
Oeters, Martin,	During the war,	K.
Otey, E. T.,	1861,	B.
Otey, G. G., Adjutant,	1861, transferred,	F. & S.
O'Gorman, Owen, Sergeant,	1861–62, discharged,	C.
Paine, J. W.,	1862–63, killed,	H.
Paine, Pleasant,	1863, to the end,	G.
Pairo, C. H.,	1861, transferred,	H.
Palmer, William H., Major,	1861–62, Adj.-Gen'l,	D. & F. & S.
Paris, Samuel A.,	First year,	E.
Parker, C. L., Corporal,	1861–64, disabled,	I.
Parker, William H., Sergeant,	1861, discharged,	B.
Patrick, ——,	1864, transferred,	G.
Patterson, William,	1861,	G.
Patton, James H.,	1861, transferred,	H.
Paul, George W.,	1861, discharged,	K.
Paul, Herman, Lieutenant,	First year,	K.
Paul, William H.,	First year,	K.
Payne, Jesse A., Lieutenant,	During the war,	B.
Peake, William,	1861–62, discharged,	D.
Pearman, R. A.,	1861, discharged,	D.
Peddle, Benjamin,	1861, discharged,	H.
Pendleton, E.,	1862–63, died,	I.
Perrin, John,	1864, to the end,	D.
Perrin, Junius P., Sergeant,	1861–65, killed,	D.
Peters, L.,	First year,	K.
Pettit, C. L.,	During the war,	D.
Pfaff, William, Lieutenant,	First year,	K.
Phillips, William F., Jr.,	First year,	E.
Pike, H. C.,	1863–64,	I.
Pinchback, ——,	1862, to the end,	B.
Pizzini, Andrew, Jr.,	1861, discharged,	D.
Pleasants, J. Adair, Paymaster,	1861, discharged, .	F. & S.
Pleasants, ——,	1862,	B.
Pledge, Joseph W.,	1861, discharged,	B.
Plunkett, H.,	1861–62, detached,	C.
Pohle, C. R. M., Drum-Major,	First year,	Band.
Polak, Jacob R., Sergeant-Major,	1861–64, discharged,	I.
Pollard, F.,	1861,	G.
Pollard, G. W.,	1863, to the end,	C.
Pollard, Robert J.,	During the war,	B.
Potee, Thomas,	1861–62, discharged,	H.
Potts, F.,	1861, detached,	C.
Powell, A. E.,	1863, to the end,	C.

Pendergast, E. M.,	1861-62, discharged,	Co. D.
Price, R. C. Corporal,	During the war,	C.
Priddy, Ezekial,	During the war,	D.
Prince, ——,	1863-64,	G.
Pritchard, John T.	1861, discharged,	G.
Pryor, J. B.,	1861-62, discharged,	G.
Pugh, F. R.,	1864, to the end,	I.
Pulling, J.,	1863, detached,	I.
Pumphry, William F.,	During the war,	H.
Purcell, Tim.,	1861-62, killed,	C.
Puryear, John W.,	1861, transferred,	G.
Quarles, J. Thomp.,	1861,	D.
Quinn, Patrick,	1864,	I.
Rae, George A.,	First year,	H.
Rainey, Calvin,	1863, to the end,	C.
Ramsburg, Edward,	First year,	E.
Randolph, John, Corporal,	First year,	E.
Rankin, James,	1861, detached,	C.
Rankin, John,	1861, detached,	C.
Rankin, Patrick, Sergeant,	1861, killed,	C.
Rankin, Tim.,	1861, discharged,	C.
Ratcliffe, J. W.,	1861-62, killed,	B.
Raymann, L.,	1861, transferred,	K.
Raynes, A. G.,	1864, to the end,	I.
Redford, C. A.,	During the war,	G.
Redford, G. Ellis,	1861-64, disabled,	H.
Redman, B. T.,	1864,	D.
Redman, R. H.,	1864, to the end,	D.
Redmond, Michael,	1861, killed,	C.
Reeve, E. Payson, Captain,	During the war,	D.
Regan, John,	1863, to the end,	I.
Reidt, P.,	First year,	K.
Reilly, J. C.,	First year,	E.
Reilly, P. K.,	First year,	E.
Reilly, P. S.,	1862, to the end,	B.
Reynolds, S. W.,	1861, detached,	G.
Richards, C. E.,	1861, detached,	B.
Richards, George H.,	1861, discharged,	H.
Richter, Robert,	First year,	K.
Rick, Joseph,	First year,	K.
Riddick, James E., Lieutenant,	1861, resigned,	G.
Riddick, Thomas S., Sergeant,	During the war,	H.
Robertson, Theo. J.,	1861-64, disabled,	D.
Robins, Logan S., Lieutenant,	During the war,	B.
Robinson, H. R.,	1861,	I.
Robinson, J. E.,	1861,	I.

Robinson, William,	First year,	Co. E.
Roby, H. R.,	1861, discharged,	I.
Rodins, John,	First year,	K.
Rogers, John T., Lieutenant,	1861, resigned,	I.
Rogers, Thomas S.,	During the war,	G.
Rommel, J. A.,	1861, discharged,	K.
Rooney, A. J.,	1861, discharged,	B.
Rose, J. H.,	1862, to the end,	H.
Rosenberger, J. A.,	First year,	Band.
Rosenberger, Laurence,	First year,	Band.
Rosenberger, Ph.,	First year,	Band.
Royster, James A.,	During the war,	G.
Royster, N. L.,	During the war,	G.
Rudd, A.,	1862, disabled,	I.
Rudd, B.,	1862,	I.
Rudd, W.,	1862,	I.
Ryan, Thomas, Sergeant,	First year,	C.
Ryan, Tim.,	1861, detached,	C.
Ryan, William, Corporal,	1861,	C.
St. Clair, ——,	1862-63, killed,	H.
Salomon, H.,	First year,	Drummer.
Samanni, F. R.,	First year,	D.
Sargent, ——, Assistant Surgeon,	1862, to the end,	F. & S.
Saunders, Joseph,	1861-63, discharged,	D.
Saunders, J. W.,	1862,	B.
Scammell, J. E.,	1863, to the last,	C.
Schad, A.,	1861,	B.
Schonborn, C. B.,	1861,	B.
Schuman, Charles,	First year,	Band.
Scherrer, P. V.,	1861, discharged,	G.
Schleisher, G.,	1861, discharged,	G.
Seagles, M., Lieutenant,	1861, resigned,	C.
Self, G. R.,	1861, to the end,	C.
Sengstack, C. P.,	First year,	E.
Senior, Thomas,	1862, transferred,	I.
Shaffer, F. B., Captain,	1861, Co. tempor'ly detach'd,	F.
Shapdock, S.,	First year,	K.
Sharp, James P.,	During the war,	G.
Sharp, Thomas L.,	During the war.	G.
Sheckell, M.,	First year,	E.
Shell, Lee R., Lieutenant,	During the war,	G.
Sheppard, ——,	1863,	H.
Sherman, Charles K., Captain,	First year,	E.
Sherman, John S.,	First year,	E.
Shiflett, J. T.,	1861-62, killed,	B.
Shortel, M.,	First year,	C.

Shumaker, G. W.,	1861, detached,	Co. I.
Shumaker, Joseph,	First year,	Drummer.
Simms, O.,	1864,	H.
Simpson, A. J. Sergeant-Major,	During the war,	D.
Sinnott, John J.,	During the war,	H.
Skinner, Fred. G., Colonel,	1861-62, disabled,	F. & S.
Sloan, L. H.,	1863,	C.
Smith, ——,	1861, died,	K.
Smith, Adam,	1862, prisoner,	B.
Smith, F.,	1863, prisoner and disabled,	H.
Smith, James,	First year,	E.
Smith, James B., (Leader),	First year,	Band.
Smith, J. H.,	1861-62, killed,	I.
Smith, L. R.,	1861-62, killed,	D.
Smith, Robert J.,	1865, to the end,	I.
Smith, W. H. C.,	1861-63,	H.
Smith, Wm. P.,	During the war,	I.
Smeltzer, J. H.,	1863,	C.
Smither's, James W.,	1861, detached,	D.
Smyth, Thomas,	First year,	E.
Snead, A. J., Corporal,	1861-62,	G.
Snow, J. R.,	1863, transferred,	I.
Snyder, John F.,	1865, to the end,	B.
Spraggins, John,	1862,	G.
Spraggins, W. S.,	1861-62, detailed,	G.
Spencer, S. B., Corporal,	First year,	E.
Spickard, H. L.,	1862, to the end,	B.
Staab, Ph.,	First year,	K.
Stach, G.,	First year,	C.
Stacy, C. B.,	1861, discharged,	B.
Stadelhofer, M.,	First year,	K.
Stagg, James,	During the war,	B.
Steger, A. G.,	During the war,	D.
Steger, E. J.,	1864,	D.
Steger, J. R.,	During the war,	D.
Steine, Simon,	First year,	E.
Stephan, Chr.,	First year,	K.
Stern, George,	First year,	I.
Stern, Samuel,	First year,	E.
Stewart, C. D.,	1862,	D.
Stewart, W. H.,	1861-62, detached,	D.
Stockton, John N. C., Adjutant,	1862, to the end,	F. & S.
Stoeber, W. A., Corporal,	1861-64, killed,	B.
Stuart, Ro. G.,	1861-62, discharged,	G.
Strang, George W.,	First year,	Drummer.
Stratton, J. L. R.,	1861, died,	H.

Stratton, Thomas E., Sergeant,	1861, transferred,	Co. B.
Straus, Robert,	First year,	B.
Strausberger, H.,	First year,	D.
Street, R. H.,	During the war,	B.
Street, Willis,	First year,	Drummer.
Strom, L. H., Corporal,	1861-62, killed,	B.
Sublett, C. M.,	1863, to the end,	D.
Sullings, Granger,	1862, to the end,	B.
Sullivan, Dan.,	1861, discharged,	C.
Sullivan, Henry, Sergeant,	1861-62, killed,	C.
Sullivan, William H.,	First year,	E.
Sullivan, John, Lieutenant,	1861, resigned,	C.
Sullivan, Pat. H.,	1861, discharged,	C.
Sullivan, William,	1861,	B.
Sutliffe, J. S.,	1861,	B.
Sweeney, ——,	1861, discharged,	I.
Sweeney, W. F.,	First year,	Drummer.
Swords, Robert D.,	1861-62, killed,	H.
Smith, Savage,	1861, detached,	G.
Tabb, J. W., Captain,	1861-62, killed,	I.
Tabb, R. L., Corporal,	1861-62, killed,	I.
Taliaferro, C. C.,	1861-62, killed,	G.
Taliaferro, E.,	1861-63, killed,	I.
Taliaferro, W. C.,	1861-63, prisoner,	I.
Tallard, C. F.,	1861-62, discharged,	I.
Tate, James,	1861-62, discharged,	B.
Taylor, J. V.,	First year,	E.
Taylor, George W.,	First year,	E.
Taylor, W. O., Captain,	1861, resigned,	I.
Terry, John,	1861,	B.
Terry, William F., Sergeant,	During the war,	I.
Thomas, L. R.,	First year,	H.
Thomas, James,	1863, to the end,	C.
Thomas, William,	First year,	E.
Thorp, John N.,	First year,	H.
Thorp, J. A.,	1863, to the end,	C.
Tieling, ——, Chaplain,	1861,	F. & S.
Tilghman, J.,	1862,	B.
Tillman, J. W.,	1863, to the end,	C.
Tinsley, C. C., Sergeant,	1861, discharged,	I.
Toler, H.,	1862,	H.
Tolker, G.,	1861, transferred,	K.
Tompkins, J.,	1861,	C.
Toomly, Jerry, Corporal,	1861-64, killed,	B.
Totty, R. T.,	First year,	B.
Tower, Isaac S., Sergeant,	1861, discharged,	B.

Towers, James E.,	First year,	Co. H.
Traylor, Thomas E., Sergeant,	During the war,	I.
Traylor, Thomas W.,	1863, to the end,	D.
Tremer, William,	First year,	Band.
Truman, A.,	1863, to the end,	C.
Tucker, A. J., Lieutenant,	1861, resigned,	G.
Tucker, Robert L.,	1861, detached,	G
Tucker, S. J., Sergeant,	1861, detached,	G.
Turner, W. W.,	During the war,	D.
Tyler, William,	1864, to the end,	B.
Tyree, James T.,	1861,	I.
Tyree, John A., Lieutenant,	First year,	I.
Tyree, Robert F.,	1861–62, killed,	G.
Tysinger, W. E., Captain,	1861–62, killed,	H.
Tyrrell, Patrick,	1861,	C.
Underhill, ——,	1864,	G.
Van Deventer, E.,	1861–62, discharged,	I.
Van Riper, John,	During the war,	D.
Vaughan, A. Jeff.,	During the war,	G.
Vaughan, James T., Lieutenant,	First year,	H.
Vaughan, John M.,	1861, transferred,	G.
Vaughan, Robert P.,	1861, discharged,	G.
Vaughan, W. J.,	1863, killed,	H.
Vermillara, P. J.,	1861, discharged,	B.
Via, J. A., Corporal,	1861–64, killed,	H.
Via, James T.,	1861, discharged,	G.
Viereok, John,	First year,	K.
Voegler, H.,	1861, discharged,	G.
Wachter, Jacob,	First year,	K.
Waddill, W. S.,	1863, killed,	H.
Waddy, George T.,	1861, detached,	D.
Wade, J.,	1863–65, killed	H.
Waggoner, D. B.,	1863–64, died,	D.
Wagner, John,	1861, detached,	K.
Wail, John,	First year,	E.
Walker, John,	1862,	I.
Walker, ——,	1863–64, died,	D.
Wallis, James B.,	1863,	I.
Walthall, H. M.,	During the war,	D.
Walthall, Ro. R.,	1861–64, killed,	G.
Wamack, J. T.,	1863,	D.
Warrolew, Joseph,	1861, transferred,	C.
Ware, William S.,	1861–62, transferred,	G.
Waters, W. G.,	First year,	E.
Watkins, Abner J., Captain,	During the war,	H.
Watkins, Thomas,	1864, to the end,	G.

Watson, H. W.,	1864, to the end,	Co. D.
Watson, ——,	1863,	H.
Webster, George,	First year,	E.
Weidenhahn, Aug., Corporal,	1861-62, disabled & disch'g'd,	K.
Weinburg, M. P.,	1861, discharged,	B.
Weller, Joseph,	1861, transferred,	H.
Wells, M. L.,	First year,	E.
Wells, Henry,	1861, discharged,	G.
Welch, M.,	1862,	I.
Werner, A.,	First year,	K.
Wesley, J. R.,	1863-64, killed,	I.
West, F. A.,	1861-62, detached,	B.
West, George L.,	1861, transferred,	B.
Westmoreland, W. A.,	1863, to the end,	D.
Weston, George E.,	1861, discharged,	H.
Wheat, N. F.,	During the war,	D.
Wheeley, C.,	1864, to the end,	D.
Wheeley, J. F.,	During the war,	D.
Whittacker, Jos. L.,	During the war,	C.
Whiting, L. A.,	1861-62, detached,	B.
White, John,	1861,	D.
White, Thomas,	1861,	G.
White, William T., Sergeant,	During the war,	I.
White, E. L.,	1863, to the end,	C.
Wiels, John,	First year,	E.
Wight, W. M.,	1861-62, killed,	H.
Wilkins, W R.,	1862, to the end,	D.
Wilkinson, George A.,	1862, to the end,	G.
Wilkinson, John K.,	During the war,	G.
Wilkinson, S. S.,	1861, killed,	G.
Wilks, W. C.,	1863,	D.
Williams, C. C.,	1863, to the end,	D.
Williams, Lewis B., Colonel,	1862-63, killed,	F. & S.
Williams, H. L.,	1863, to the end,	C.
Williams, T. J.,	1864, died,	H.
Williams, A. J.,	1863, to the end,	C.
Wills, C. A.,	1863-64, killed,	I.
Wills, S.,	1863, discharged,	I.
Wilson, James W.,	1861,	B.
Wilson, Robert B.,	1861, discharged,	H.
Wilzinski, L.,	1861-62, discharged,	H.
Winfree, John M.,	1861-62, detached,	G.
Wingfield, L. R.,	During the war,	D.
Wingfield, M. J.,	1861-63, killed,	D.
Wingfield, Samuel L.,	During the war,	D.
Wingo, W. W.,	1862, detached,	I.

Wingo, Charles E.,	1861, transferred,	Co. D.
Winter, John,	1861, detached,	K.
Witzlieben, T. A.,	First year,	E.
Wolfe, Henry,	1861,	B.
Womack, Robert E.,	1862, to the end,	H.
Wood, R.,	1863,	I.
Wood, William A.,	1862, to the end,	G.
Wood, ——,	1863,	H.
Woods, Joseph,	1861-62, discharged,	C.
Woods, Patrick, Sergeant,	During the war,	C.
Woody, William T., Lieutenant,	During the war,	G.
Word, B. H.,	1864, to the end,	D.
Worrell, W. J. G.,	1863,	C.
Wren, Powhatan,	1861-62, discharged,	D.
Wright, Elijah G., Sergeant,	During the war,	G.
Wright, John T.,	1861, discharged,	B.
Wynne, John W., Sergeant,	1861-64, killed,	H.
Yancey, John K.,	1863-64, disabled,	I.
Young, M.,	1863,	D.
Youell, Robert,	1863,	C.
Zimmerman, A. M.,	First year,	E.

www.ingramcontent.com/pod-product-compliance
Lightning Source LLC
Chambersburg PA
CBHW032351020726
47499CB00008B/2701